THE SAN LUIS OBISPO FARMERS' MARKET COOKBOOK

Simple Seasonal Recipes & Short Stories from the Central Coast of California

Thankful for the farmers that make our recipes so delicious!
xo,
Kendra Arons

KENDRA ARONSON

slofarmersmarketcookbook.com

KENDRA ARONSON
Writer, Photographer,
Designer, Self-publisher
kendraaronson.com

SHEA SOMMA
Editor-in-Chief

GLORIA ARONSON
Recipe Editor

Printed in Canada.
Hemlock Printers
hemlock.com

MIX Paper from responsible sources FSC® C014956

zero 100% carbon neutral by Hemlock Printers www.hemlock.com/zero

Greenhouse gas emissions from the paper lifecycle, the transport, and the printing of this item have been offset through investments in energy efficiency and non-fossil fuel energy technologies.

PHOTO CREDIT: CANA FAMILY.

DEDICATION

MAMA

Thank you for always insisting we gather around the dinner table every evening to share your delicious homemade meals. Thank you for teaching me how important it is to nourish the stomach with good food and the soul with good community.

DADDY-O

Thank you for always encouraging me to chase my dreams—both the realistic and far-fetched ones—for providing insightful, constructive criticism, and for motivating me to always produce the highest caliber work on every project I tackle.

BRUDDER

Thank you for always being an inventive and productive human being; your ability to put thoughts into actions is very inspiring. You were instrumental in my Kickstarter campaign—your input, advice, and guidance continue to be invaluable.

MY SHEA

Thank you for always believing in my creative pursuits, for cheering me on in my entrepreneurial journey, and for being my editorial eagle eye. This cookbook could not have happened without you supporting me every step of the way—you are the world's most patient, generous, and kind husband. I love you so much.

FARMERS

You are the unsung heroes of the Central Coast—without you we would all be hungry! Thank you for dedicating your lives to cultivating the wonderful variety of Earth's treasures.

FOOD ARTISANS & CHEFS

You are the champions of the local, seasonal food movement. Thank you for playing a pivotal role in exciting my palette by utilizing the freshest fruits, vegetables, cheeses, eggs, fish, poultry, and meats.

KICKSTARTER BACKERS

Without your generous pledges and pre-orders, this cookbook would not be the tangible reality you now hold in your hands. I am eternally grateful that you invested in my personal project. I hope you enjoy it!

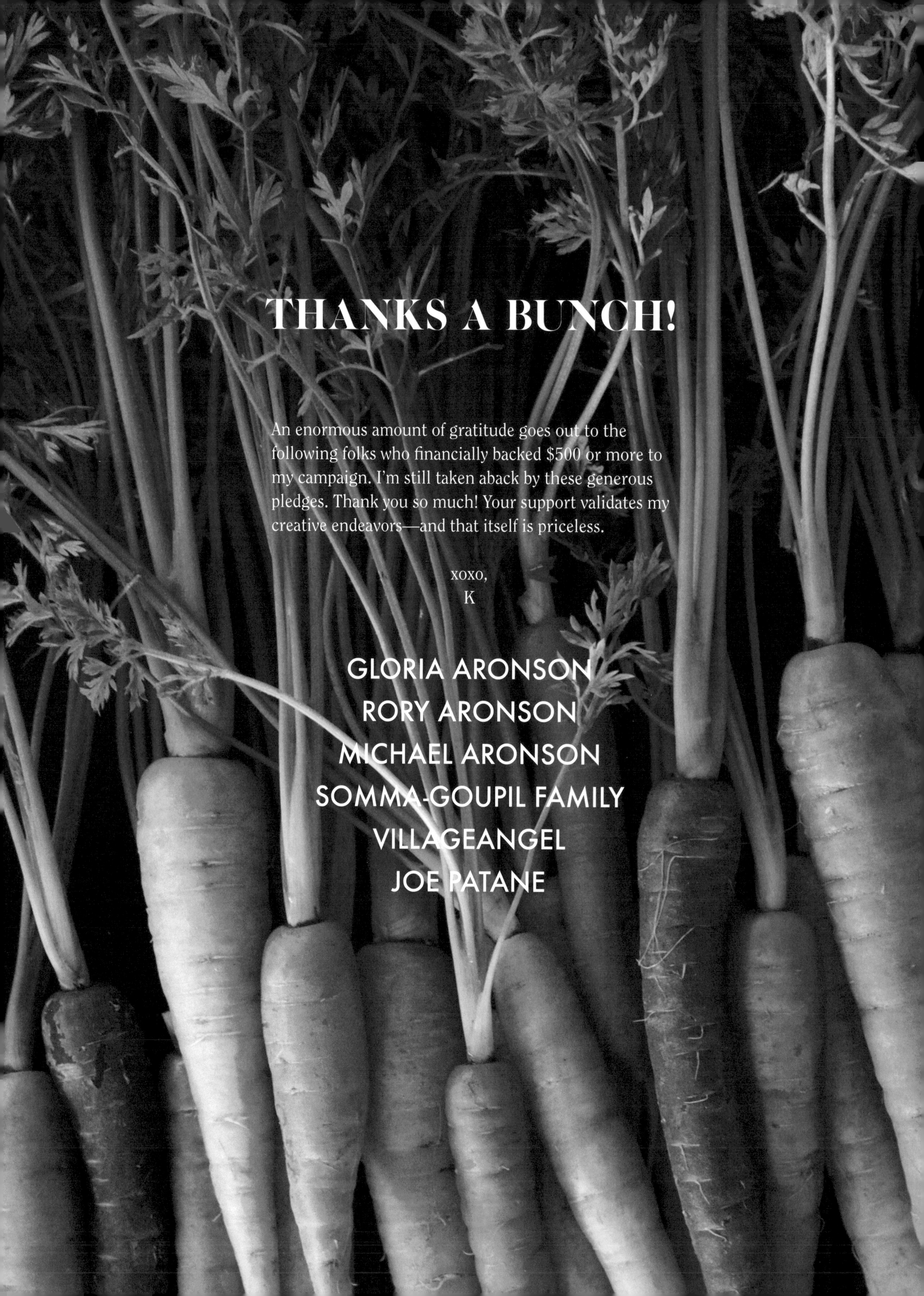

THANKS A BUNCH!

An enormous amount of gratitude goes out to the following folks who financially backed $500 or more to my campaign. I'm still taken aback by these generous pledges. Thank you so much! Your support validates my creative endeavors—and that itself is priceless.

xoxo,
K

GLORIA ARONSON
RORY ARONSON
MICHAEL ARONSON
SOMMA-GOUPIL FAMILY
VILLAGEANGEL
JOE PATANE

TABLE OF CONTENTS

INSPIRATION FOR WRITING

My name is Kendra Aronson, so nice to meet you! I'm the writer, photographer, designer, and self-publisher of *The San Luis Obispo Farmers' Market Cookbook: Simple Seasonal Recipes & Short Stories from the Central Coast of California*. Three years ago I embarked on this creative journey to create a community keepsake that would inspire others to shake hands with their SLOcal farmers, to cook simple seasonal recipes, and to support restaurants sharing the farm-to-table mission.

With over 120 vendors each week, the downtown Thursday evening San Luis Obispo farmers' market is one of the finest, most established, and longest-lasting markets in the nation. Additionally, San Luis Obispo County boasts 20 weekly farmers' markets (p. 8–9) with hard-working folks committed to bringing only the freshest and most delicious produce, meats, fish, cheeses, breads, and more to County residents. This was the catalyst that compelled me to create this cookbook celebrating both the weekly bounty and the stories of these producers.

As I started to frequent the other SLO markets—the Saturday morning market off Dalidio Drive and the Tuesday afternoon market on Broad Street—I began to get to know the amazing people who provide such tasty, nourishing ingredients for my weekly seasonal meals. There is Julia Gomez of Julia's Juices (p. 161), who sources her fruits and vegetables from both her husband Javier Magaña's farm, Red Barn Farms (p. 175), and her sister's farm, Bautista Farms (p. 151). Oftentimes the produce is picked early morning, juiced mid-morning, and sold at market that same afternoon or evening. You'd be hard-pressed (pun intended!) to find a fresher farm-to-glass juice operation anywhere. Then there is Philip Langston of SLO Grown Produce (p. 184), who grows the most beautiful, bright, juicy tomatoes year-round. As a Cal Poly Crop Science major in the 80s, Philip had dreams of working for NASA to grow plants in outer space—he was fascinated by seed germination in simulated weightlessness. He now grows multiple varieties of tomatoes, eggplants, cucumbers, and basil in his half-acre greenhouse. He is able to grow so much by scaling up vertically on vining tracks rather than horizontally on the ground, and by utilizing a hydroponic system as a method of growing his precious produce. It is truly a sight to see!

SLO County also hosts a huge array of world-class dining. The chefs that prepare these feasts rely on the freshest ingredients locally available to create their dishes. Multiple times a week I see Market Manager Matt Kubat, whose full-time job is sourcing for Robin's Restaurant (p. 178–179), Novo Restaurant & Lounge (p. 170–171), and Luna Red Restaurant • Bar (p. 164). Crates upon crates brimming with freshly-picked produce are delivered to these three fine establishments on a daily basis—sometimes twice a day to keep up with the demand of these high volume restaurants. Brandon Manuele of Sally Loo's (p. 181) and Brian Collins of Ember Restaurant (p. 157) are also frequent market shoppers seen sourcing the week's harvest. It's incredible to see all the dedication that goes into upholding a farm-to-table mission.

It's the stories of farmers, food artisans, and chefs like these that I want everyone to hear. My cookbook features seasonal recipes and short stories about these amazing individuals who play a significant part in bringing food to our tables. The recipes are organized by seasons (15 recipes per season) and are sub-divided into five categories: breakfast, light bites, lunch, dinner, and dessert (3 recipes per category). In the spirit of collaboration, the majority of the recipes are provided by these fine food folks around the County in order to showcase the true taste of the Central Coast.

Like any huge endeavor, it takes a village. In order to self-publish this cookbook, I ran a month-long campaign raising funds for the up-front printing costs. $26,714 was raised on Kickstarter, an incredible crowdfunding platform that brings creative projects to life. This cookbook would not exist without these generous pledges and pre-order sales. I am truly blown away by the outpouring of support—if you financially backed this campaign, I can not thank you enough for believing in me! I poured my heart into this cookbook; I hope you love it, too! —XOXO, KENDRA

PHOTO CREDIT: JOE JOHNSTON PHOTOGRAPHY.

COOKBOOK GUIDE

ABBREVIATIONS

t. = teaspoons
T = tablespoons
oz. = ounces
lbs. = pounds

INGREDIENT SUGGESTIONS

The best food comes from simple ingredients. Whenever cited, please use the following:

salt = kosher salt
pepper = freshly cracked black pepper
eggs = free range organic eggs
milk = organic whole milk
butter = organic unsalted butter
olive oil = high-quality extra-virgin

HOW TO GET THE MOST OUT OF THIS COOKBOOK

Some recipes do not have exact measurements, so make sure to read the recipe in its entirety to get an idea of what to do. Remember: it's not rocket science—it's food! If it makes you feel any better, I myself have no formal culinary training. If I can do it, you can do it. Have fun, get messy, and feel free to share your meals with the hashtag: #slofarmersmarketcookbook

WEEKLY FARMERS' MARKETS

BAYWOOD/LOS OSOS
MONDAY AFTERNOONS
2 p.m.-4:30 p.m.
2nd Street & Santa Maria Street
93402 » near the Bay

PISMO BEACH
TUESDAY MORNINGS
8:30 a.m.-11:30 a.m.
555 5 Cities Drive & N. 4th Street
93449 » near the 101 freeway

PASO ROBLES
TUESDAY AFTERNOONS
3 p.m.-6 p.m.
11th Street & Spring Street
93446 » in the City Park

SAN LUIS OBISPO
TUESDAY AFTERNOONS
3 p.m.-6 p.m.
Broad Street & Stoneridge Drive
93401 » at the SLO Grange Hall

ARROYO GRANDE
WEDNESDAY MORNINGS
8:30 a.m.-11 a.m.
E. Grand Avenue & Courtland Street
93420 » in the Smart & Final parking lot

ATASCADERO
WEDNESDAY AFTERNOONS
3 p.m.-6 p.m.
El Camino Real & Curbaril Avenue
93422 » in the El Camino Real Plaza shopping center lot

PISMO BEACH
WEDNESDAY AFTERNOONS
3 p.m.-7 p.m.
2 p.m.-5 p.m. (DST)
Main Street & Dolliver Street
93449 » near the Pismo Pier

MORRO BAY
THURSDAY AFTERNOONS
2:30 p.m.-5 p.m.
Main Street & Pico Street
93442 » in the Spencer's parking lot

SAN LUIS OBISPO
THURSDAY EVENINGS
6 p.m.-9 p.m.
Downtown SLO
93401 » on the main drag of Higuera Street

CAYUCOS*
FRIDAY MORNINGS
10 a.m.-12:30 p.m.
Ocean Avenue & Cayucos Drive
93430 » in the Vets Hall parking lot
*Seasonal market:
Memorial Day—Labor Day

CAMBRIA
FRIDAY AFTERNOONS
2:30 p.m.-5 p.m. (November—April)
2:30 p.m.-5:30 p.m. (May—October)
Main Street & Cambria Road
93428 » Veteran's Memorial parking lot

AVILA BEACH*
FRIDAY EVENINGS
4 p.m.-8 p.m.
Promenade on Front Street
93424 » near the Avila Pier
*Seasonal market:
mid-April—mid-September

SAN LUIS OBISPO
SATURDAY MORNINGS
8 a.m.-10:45 a.m.
Dalidio Drive
93405 » Cost Plus parking lot

PASO ROBLES
SATURDAY MORNINGS
9 a.m.-1 p.m.
11th Street & Spring Street
93446 » in the City Park

TEMPLETON
SATURDAY MORNINGS
9 a.m.-12:30 p.m.
6th Street & Crocker Street
93465 » in the City Park

ARROYO GRANDE
SATURDAY AFTERNOONS
12 p.m.-2:30 p.m.
Olohan Alley & Short Street
93420 » in the Centennial Park

MORRO BAY
SATURDAY AFTERNOONS
3 p.m.-6 p.m.
2 p.m.-5 p.m. (DST)
Main Street & Harbor Street
93442 » downtown Morro Bay

SAN LUIS OBISPO
SUNDAY MORNINGS
10 a.m.-2 p.m.
Tank Farm Road & Long Street
93401 » in the Kennedy Fitness parking lot

NIPOMO
SUNDAY AFTERNOONS
11:30 a.m.-2:30 p.m.
Trilogy Parkway & Via Concha Road
93444 » in the Monarch Country Club

GROVER BEACH*
SUNDAY AFTERNOONS
3 p.m.-6 p.m.
10th Street & Ramona Avenue
93433 » in the Ramona Garden Park
*Seasonal market:
June—September

MARKET TOTE

This double-sided 15" x 20" market tote bag is both beautiful and functional. The front of the tote showcases a map of San Luis Obispo County and its 20 weekly farmers' markets. The market information—locations, dates, and times—is displayed on the back.

The canvas is thick, hefty, and durable. Don't forget to bring this reusable tote to the markets when bringing home your seasonal haul!

MARKET MAP

This 14" x 20" letterpress market map highlights the 20 weekly farmers' markets in San Luis Obispo County. The market information—locations, dates, and times—is displayed below the halftone map in chronological order with a corresponding red pin. The thick texturized paper has the feel of fabric which accentuates the sexy letterpress impression. This market map would look great on any wall space—framed or unframed!

Both items are available for purchase at:
slofarmersmarketcookbook.com

BREAKFAST

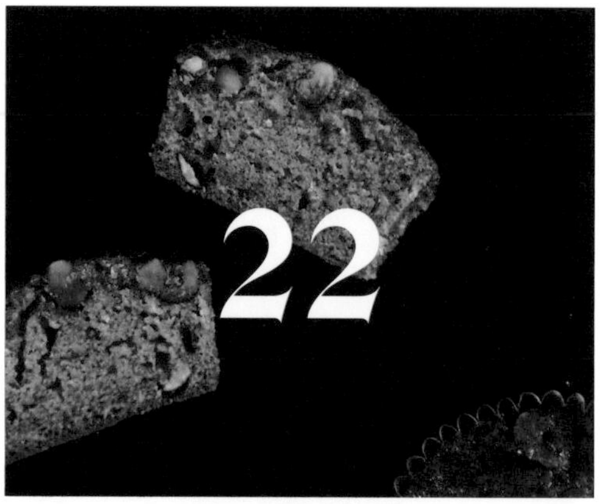

LIGHT BITES

LUNCH

DINNER

DESSERT

BREAKFAST

LIGHT BITES

LUNCH

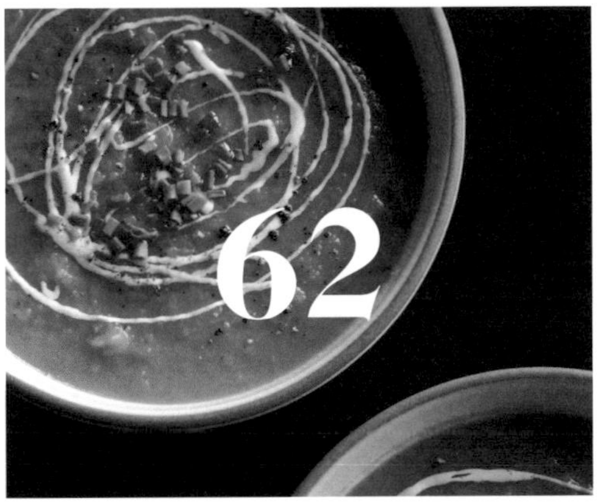

DINNER

DESSERT

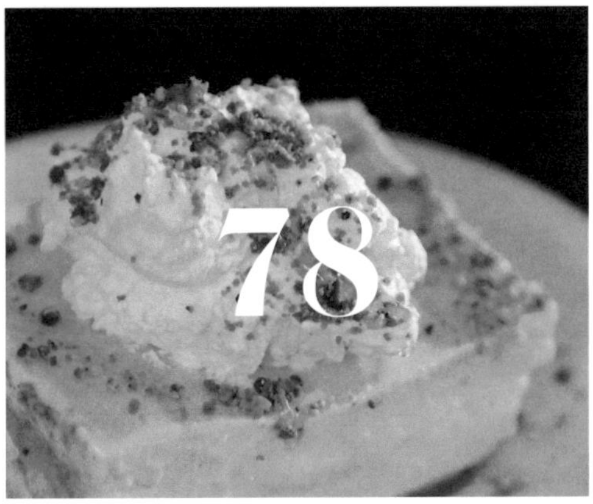

BREAKFAST

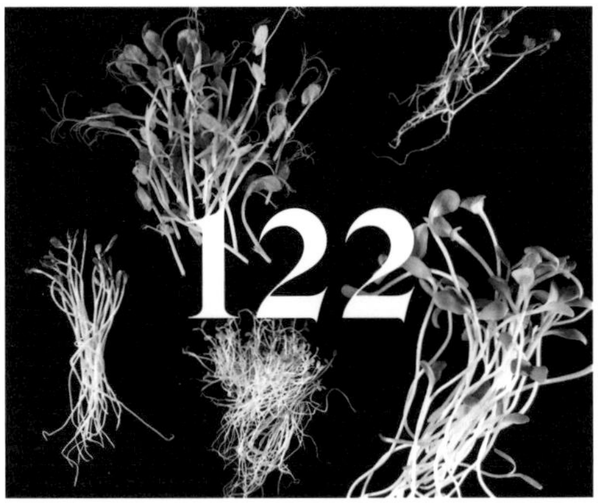

LIGHT BITES

LUNCH

DINNER

DESSERT

SHORT STORIES

MAMA'S PRESERVES
Lori Heal
Arroyo Grande
166

MEZE WINE BAR & BISTRO
Lisa & John Schiltz
San Luis Obispo
167

MT. OLIVE ORGANIC FARM
Ng Family
Paso Robles
168

NEGRANTI CREAMERY
Alexis Negranti
Paso Robles
169

NOVO RESTAURANT & LOUNGE
Ben Richardson
San Luis Obispo
170

NOVO RESTAURANT & LOUNGE
Robin Covey
San Luis Obispo
171

OLD SLO BBQ
Matt Pearce
San Luis Obispo
172

PC CATTLE CO.
Jordin & Pete Cramer
San Luis Obispo
173

PEPPER CREEK FAMILY FARMS
Boyd Family
Arroyo Grande
174

RED BARN FARMS
Javier Magaña
Arroyo Grande
175

RIGHETTI RANCH
Righetti Family
San Luis Obispo
176

RINCONADA DAIRY
Christine & Jim Maguire
Santa Margarita
177

ROBIN'S RESTAURANT
Shanny Covey
Cambria
178

ROBIN'S RESTAURANT
William Ouderkirk
Cambria
179

RUTIZ FAMILY FARMS
Jerry Rutiz
Arroyo Grande
180

SALLY LOO'S
Jen & Brandon Manuele
San Luis Obispo
181

SCOUT COFFEE CO.
Sara & Jon Peterson
San Luis Obispo
182

SLO CREEK FARMS
Gable Family
San Luis Obispo
183

SLO GROWN PRODUCE & LONE OAK OLIVE OIL
Philip & Nancy Langston
Arroyo Grande
184

THE SPOON TRADE
Jacob & Brooke Town, Patrick Bergseid
Grover Beach
185

SWEET PEA BAKERY
Kelli Castle
Arroyo Grande
186

TALLEY FARMS
Andrea Chavez
Arroyo Grande
187

THOMAS HILL ORGANICS
Chris Manning
Paso Robles
188

Y. HAYASHI & SONS FARMS
Hayashi Family
Arroyo Grande
189

SUMMER

STRAWBERRY PANCAKES WITH VANILLA MAPLE GLAZE

These pancakes are bursting with sweetness—the sliced strawberries, the vanilla and maple glaze, and the light dusting of powdered sugar make this stack a total knockout. Invite your friends over for a decadent Sunday brunch!

PANCAKES

6 eggs
1 cup whole milk
1 cup buttermilk
½ cup vegetable oil
1 t. vanilla extract
4 cups all-purpose flour
1 cup granulated sugar
2 T baking powder
1 T active dry yeast
pinch of salt
unsalted butter
strawberries, sliced

VANILLA MAPLE GLAZE

1 cup powdered sugar, sifted
¼ cup unsalted butter, melted
½ cup maple syrup
1 t. vanilla extract

PANCAKES

In a bowl, beat the eggs well. Whisk in wet ingredients: milk, buttermilk, vegetable oil, and vanilla extract. In a separate bowl, mix together the dry ingredients through a sifter. This will eliminate any lumps in the flour and will result in fluffy pancakes.

Incorporate wet ingredients from the first bowl into the dry ingredients' bowl. Pour slowly and mix gently until batter is combined. There will be a few lumps, but don't worry—they will cook out. Do not overmix the batter.

On a non-stick pan or griddle, set the temperature to medium-low heat. Once it's heated, butter up the surface. With a measuring cup, pour ½ cup of batter to make uniform pancakes. It will take a couple of minutes per side. Once little bubbles appear on the surface, take a peek to see if the bottom is golden brown, then flip to cook the other side. Serve immediately or pop them on a baking tray in the oven at 200°F to keep the batch warm. Between batches, wipe down cooking surface with a paper napkin and add more butter as needed.

VANILLA MAPLE GLAZE

Sift powdered sugar into a small bowl. Pour in melted butter, maple syrup, and vanilla extract. Whisk together until smooth.

» Now comes the fun part: plating! Stack your pancakes up, slice your strawberries, drizzle with the vanilla and maple sugar glaze, and lightly dust with sifted powdered sugar.

RECIPE CONTRIBUTED BY
Chef Liz Lynch

ALMOND COCONUT BLUEBERRY SCONES & ALMOND MILK

These blueberry scones are irresistibly flaky and bursting with fruit. Enjoy with almond milk two ways—chilled over ice for a light, smooth experience or steamed up in a thick, creamy espresso drink.

ALMOND MILK
almonds
water
salt
local wildflower honey

ALMOND COCONUT BLUEBERRY SCONES
¾ cup almond meal
¼ cup coconut flour
¼ cup arrowroot flour
¼ cup toasted shredded coconut
2 T cane sugar
¾ t. salt
2 t. baking powder, sifted
½ t. baking soda, sifted
6 oz. cold butter, cubed
⅔ cup heavy cream
1 egg yolk
1 t. vanilla paste
1 pint blueberries

VANILLA BEAN GLAZE
half of a vanilla bean
¼ cup milk
2 cups powdered sugar

Yields 8 scones.

RECIPE CONTRIBUTED BY
Sara Peterson
Scout Coffee Co. (p. 182)

ALMOND MILK

This recipe is about ratios, so make as much or as little as you want! Soak almonds overnight in water—feel free to refrigerate or leave them out on your counter.

The next morning, rinse the almonds. Then, in a blender, combine one part soaked almond with 3 parts filtered water. Add a pinch of salt and a squeeze of honey. Blend for 20-30 seconds. Pour the mixture through a cheesecloth over a bowl; then squeeze as much liquid out as possible. Store the finished almond milk in a glass bottle in the fridge (will keep up to 5 days). You can save the remaining pulp for almond meal as the base of the scones below.

ALMOND COCONUT BLUEBERRY SCONES

Lay the soaked almonds on a parchment-lined sheet pan and dehydrate in the oven at 200°F for 2 hours. Then run through a grain mill (or food processor) to make the mixture a bit finer in order to better incorporate into the pastry dough. Approximately 1 cup of almonds (soaked from the almond milk recipe above) will yield ¾ cup almond meal.

Combine dry ingredients in a mixing bowl. Cut in the butter. Tip from Sara, Baker/Owner of Scout Coffee Co. (p. 182): "I do this first with a pastry cutter, then I do this with my hands, almost as if I am making a pie crust. Try to get all the 'flour' buttery and leave a few chunks."

In a separate bowl, combine wet ingredients; stir well. Add these wet ingredients to the crumbly buttery "flour" mixture. Fold in bluberries.

Turn the dough out onto a work surface. Pat into a circle, about 9 inches round and cut into 8 wedges. Place scones on a parchment paper-lined pan, pop in the freezer for 20 minutes. Then bake at 325°F for 25–27 minutes.

VANILLA BEAN GLAZE

Scrape the inside of the vanilla bean. Whisk together the vanilla, milk, and powdered sugar until smooth. Once scones are cool, drizzle on the glaze.

» Enjoy the warm scones with a nice glass of almond milk!

SPICED ZUCCHINI MUFFINS WITH WALNUTS & HAZELNUTS

These muffins are an absolute cinch to make. The zucchini, walnuts, and hazelnuts make these muffins hefty, dense, and quite filling. They make for great hiking snacks or post-workout fuel!

MUFFINS

1 cup zucchini, grated
2 eggs, beaten
½ cup olive oil
1 cup flour
1 cup brown sugar
pinch of salt
½ t. baking powder
⅓ t. baking soda
½ t. cinnamon
⅓ cup walnuts, halved
⅓ cup hazelnuts, halved
⅓ t. allspice
pinch of nutmeg, grated

MUFFINS

Preheat oven to 350°F. Combine zucchini, eggs, and olive oil in a bowl. Mix thoroughly with a wooden spoon.

In a separate bowl, mix together remaining ingredients: flour, sugar, salt, baking powder, baking soda, cinnamon, nuts, allspice, and nutmeg. Once thoroughly mixed, add this dry mixture to the wet ingredients.
Mix everything together.

Line a muffin tray with muffin liners. Distribute muffin dough among the cups, filling each individual cup to the brim. Bake for 45 minutes on the middle rack until the muffins are golden brown. Check after 30 minutes and continue to check for doneness in 5 minute intervals. [Do you know the toothpick trick? Stick a toothpick into the muffin and pull it out—if there is no dough residue on the toothpick, your muffins are done! This trick works for cupcakes as well.]

Remove muffins from the oven. Let the muffins cool in the muffin tray for 5 minutes, then remove individual muffins from the tray and let cool for another 15 minutes.

Kendra's suggestion: serve with a nice glass of cold almond milk *(p. 21).*

RECIPE CONTRIBUTED BY

Bev Dana
Y. Hayashi & Sons Farm (p. 189)

CROSTINI WITH SUNGOLDS, ZUCCHINI, BREBIS, & SPICY PESTO

This dish was inspired by a summertime Saturday morning market run—freshly baked bread, eye-popping sungolds, spicy padróns, bright green zucchini, farmstead cheeses, and crunchy nuts! A perfect appetizer for a late afternoon gathering.

PADRÓNS

olive oil
(from Lone Oak Olive Oil, p. 184)
padrón peppers
sea salt flakes

CROSTINI

zucchini, sliced and grilled
olive oil
ciabatta, sliced and grilled
sungold tomatoes, halved
fresh brebis (or chèvre)
(from Rinconada Dairy, p. 177)

SPICY PISTACHIO PESTO

$\frac{1}{3}$ cup spicy roasted pistachios
$\frac{1}{3}$ cup hard sheep's milk cheese
(from Rinconada Dairy, p. 177)
2 cups fresh basil leaves
(from SLO Grown Produce, p. 184)
5 cloves of garlic
red pepper flakes
$\frac{1}{2}$ cup olive oil
salt and pepper

PADRÓNS

Heat up a cast-iron skillet over medium-high flame. Once hot enough, add some olive oil and throw in the padrón peppers. Blister and blacken peppers, remove from heat. Sprinkle with sea salt flakes.

CROSTINI

Carefully slice zucchini on a mandolin to get thin ribbons, drizzle with olive oil and grill until tender. Once done, remove from heat and set aside for assembly. Halve sungold tomatoes, set aside for assembly. Slice and grill the ciabatta bread.

SPICY PISTACHIO PESTO

In a food processor, combine pistachios, cheese, basil, and garlic. Pulse until combined into a paste. Add pinches of salt, pepper, and red pepper flakes. Blend together and slowly drizzle in oil as it forms into a smooth sauce. Taste for seasoning and spiciness; adjust accordingly.

» Top half of the crostini with a generous amount of fresh *brebis*—this French word refers to sheep's milk, whereas *chèvre* refers to goat's milk—and halved sungolds. Top the other half of crostini with a spoonful of spicy pistachio pesto and thinly sliced grilled zucchini. Serve alongside salty padrón peppers, extra whole sungolds, and pistachios in their shells.

RECIPE CREATED BY
Kendra Aronson (p. 6)

ROASTED CAULIFLOWER OVER ARUGULA WITH AVOCADO DRESSING

This creamy avocado dressing will make you weak in the knees. Impress your friends and family with this elevated cauliflower dish at your next potluck! The extra step of pickling the fresh corn is well worth the effort.

CAULIFLOWER

1 head of cauliflower, trimmed
¼ cup olive oil
1 T. fresh thyme leaves
2 cloves of garlic, crushed
2 t. salt
arugula
Manchego cheese

PICKLED CORN

2 cups corn kernels
½ cup granulated sugar
1 cup water
2 cups white wine vinegar
¼ cup sugar
1 t. salt

AVOCADO DRESSING

½ cup fresh parsley
½ cup fresh tarragon
½ cup fresh chervil
2 avocados
2 T. dijon mustard
¼ T. lemon juice
¼ cup water
1 egg yolk
2 T. lemon oil
1 cup olive oil
1½ T salt

CAULIFLOWER

Preheat oven to 400°F. Trim the cauliflower into bite-size florets. Toss the cauliflower with the olive oil, thyme, garlic, and salt. Mix well and place onto a baking sheet. Roast at 400°F for 15–20 minutes, or until the cauliflower is tender and golden brown. Remove from oven and set aside.

PICKLED CORN

Husk your corn and remove the silk. Choose a pot large enough to boil 3 ears of corn. Boil the water with a ½ cup of sugar. With tongs, transfer the ears of corn into the boiling water. Boil for 3–8 minutes until tender crisp—soft enough to press, but not mushy. Remove from water and let sit until cool enough to handle. Slice off the kernels from the cob and place into a large mason jar.

Boil 1 cup water, vinegar, ¼ cup sugar, and salt. When the sugar and salt have dissolved, bring to a simmer. Pour the liquid over the kernels in the jar. Seal with an airtight lid. Let it cool to room temperature, then refrigerate.

AVOCADO DRESSING

Start by blanching all the herbs for 45 seconds and transfer to an ice bath. Squeeze dry and chop finely. Scoop the avocados from their skins. In a food processor, add the avocados, the finely chopped herbs, mustard, lemon juice, water, and egg yolk. Process until smooth, then stream in the lemon oil and olive oil. Add salt to taste.

» Place a generous amount of dressing on the bottom of each plate, pile on the roasted cauliflower, a handful of fresh arugula, strain the corn from the pickling liquid, and garnish with grated Manchego cheese.

RECIPE CONTRIBUTED BY

Jacob Town
The Spoon Trade (p. 185)

JERRY'S DOUBLE CITRUS ICED MINT TEA

There's nothing quite like an icy glass of sweet mint tea on a hot summer day. Personally, I love arranging slices of citrus on each glass for a fancy, yet playful presentation!

MINT TEA

4 mint tea bags
1 bunch of mint
(from Rutiz Family Farms, p. 180)
3 cups water, boiled
1 cup sugar
1 cup orange juice
¼ cup lemon juice
6 cups water
sprigs of mint
citrus slices

MINT TEA

Place tea bags and mint leaves in a 3-quart pitcher. Add 3 cups boiling water and sugar (use less than 1 cup if you don't desire a sweet tea). Stir until sugar is dissolved and steep until cool. Discard tea bags and mint leaves.

Add orange juice, lemon juice, and 6 cups of water to the tea mixture. Serve over ice; garnish with mint sprigs and citrus slices.

RECIPE CONTRIBUTED BY

Jerry Rutiz
Rutiz Family Farms (p. 180)

GRILLED SALMON WITH BROILED APRICOT JALAPEÑO PRESERVES

These sweet, spicy, and savory apricot jalapeño preserves pack an incredible flavor into this lightly grilled fish dish. Serve alongside grilled asparagus and you have yourself the ultimate summer meal!

SALMON

fillets of salmon (≈ ¾ lb. per serving)
olive oil
salt and pepper
apricot jalapeño preserves
(from Mama's Preserves, p. 166)

ASPARAGUS

1 bunch of asparagus
olive oil
salt and pepper
lemon wedges

SALMON

Fire up your grill and let it get quite hot. Drizzle olive oil over salmon fillets. Season with salt and pepper. Lower the grill to medium-high heat and grill the salmon skin-side down. Grill with the lid closed for 7–8 minutes. With a fish spatula, remove from heat and set aside on a baking tray.

ASPARAGUS

Toss the asparagus in a bowl with some olive oil, salt, and pepper. Coat evenly. On medium-high heat, grill with the lid closed for 5–7 minutes or until slightly charred and tender. Remove from the grill and place onto the baking tray with the grilled salmon.

» Set oven to broil (450°F-500°F). Pour the apricot jalapeño preserves over the grilled salmon fillets. Broil until the preserves starts to bubble and get crispy, about 1–2 minutes. Remove from oven; serve immediately with lemon wedges.

RECIPE CONTRIBUTED BY

Lori Heal
Mama's Preserves (p. 166)

NANCY'S FAVORITE PENNE PASTA WITH FRESH TOMATOES & BASIL

This pasta is the ultimate trio: simple, quick, and delicious! It's the type of dish that you can easily take to your office for lunch or whip up after a long day of work.

PASTA

penne pasta for two
¼ cup fresh basil, finely minced
(from SLO Grown Produce, p. 184)
Parmesan cheese
2 medium tomatoes, diced
(from SLO Grown Produce, p. 184)
garlic salt
black pepper or lemon pepper
olive oil
(from Lone Oak Olive Oil, p. 184)

PASTA

Boil water, cook enough penne for 2 servings, and drain.

Finely mince the fresh basil. According to Nancy, the wife of farmer Philip, "Lemon basil is a favorite. Purple opal and Italian basil combined is very appealing to the palate, as well as the eye." Dice the tomatoes.

» Place the pasta in a mixing bowl, top with basil, cheese, and tomatoes. Sprinkle on garlic salt, black pepper or lemon pepper, and drizzle with olive oil. Toss lightly. Plate and serve.

RECIPE CONTRIBUTED BY

Nancy Langston
SLO Grown Produce &
Lone Oak Olive Oil (p. 184)

CAPTAIN EVANS'-STYLE DREDGED SAND SOLE

In the summertime, I always crave lighter fare—this lightly-dredged, locally caught sand sole makes great fish sandwiches and fish tacos, or can be served by itself with some generous squeezes of lemon juice.

SAND SOLE

- sand sole
- flour
- salt and pepper
- butter
- lemons
- red pepper flakes (optional)

SAND SOLE

According to Margie Hurd of SLO Fresh Catch, the U.S. West Coast's first community supported fishery (CSF): "Travis Evans is now in his nineties and began commercial fishing during World War II when the public and troops needed fresh fish. Evans and his wife Katherine have been married over sixty years and raised eight children. Evans is considered a legend amongst San Luis Obispo County commercial fishermen."

In the words of Captain Evans, "I just put some flour, salt, and pepper in a paper bag. Then I add the fillet and shake the bag. I shake the excess flour off the fish, then I cook it in a fry pan with butter." It's that simple, folks! Sprinkle with red pepper flakes if you'd like to kick up the heat.

Although SLO Fresh Catch is no longer in operation, fish at SLOcal farmers' markets are still caught by local commercial fisherman and are now processed by Mark Tognazzini of Tognazzini's Dockside Fish Market based in Morro Bay.

RECIPE CONTRIBUTED BY

Margie Hurd (& Captain Evans)
Formerly of SLO Fresh Catch

GNOCCHI AL POMODORO

Mama's Meatball has a special place in my heart and stomach—those are one and the same, right? Keep a few jars of their marinara stocked at home in your pantry for when a pasta craving strikes!

GNOCCHI

3 lbs. russet potatoes
2 cups all-purpose flour
1 egg, extra large
1 pinch salt
1 pinch of nutmeg, grated
½ cup Parmesan cheese, grated
olive oil
marinara sauce
(from Mama's Meatball, p. 165)

GNOCCHI

Boil the whole potatoes until they are soft, about 45 minutes. While still warm, peel and pass through a vegetable mill onto a clean, flat surface. Form the potatoes into a mound.

Boil 6 quarts of water in a large spaghetti pot. Set up an ice bath with 6 cups of ice and 6 cups water near the stove top.

Make a well in the center of the potatoes and sprinkle all over with flour, using up all the flour. Place the egg, salt, nutmeg, and Parmesan in the center of well. Using a fork, stir the egg into flour and potatoes, just like making traditional pasta. Once the egg is mixed in, bring dough together, kneading gently until a ball is formed. Knead gently another 4 minutes until the ball is dry to touch.

Form the dough into a rectangular shape. With a pastry cutter, cut the dough into horizontal slices and roll into ¾-inch diameter dowels. With a pastry cutter, cut the dowels into 1-inch long pieces. Roll the individual pieces off of a fork to make small indentations; dust fork with flour if needed. Drop these pieces into the boiling water and cook until they float to the top of the boiling water, about 1 minute. Meanwhile, continue with remaining dough, forming dowels, cutting into 1-inch pieces and rolling off of the fork. As the gnocchi float to top of boiling water, remove them, and place them in the ice bath to cool down.

Drain well and toss lightly with a touch of olive oil to prevent sticking. When you are ready to serve, simply toss gnocchi with warm sauce in a saucepan—preferably Mama's Meatball marinara sauce that is available for purchase by the jar at the downtown San Luis Obispo farmers' market and their restaurant in the Creamery.

RECIPE CONTRIBUTED BY
Nicola Allegretta
Mama's Meatball (p. 165)

THE SPOON TRADE'S BURGER, PICKLED ZUCCHINI, & FRIES

Summer calls for poolside barbecues and grilled burgers. Challenge yourself with this comprehensive recipe for the all-American duo by making everything from scratch!

BREAD AND BUTTER PICKLES

1 quart water
2 cups granulated sugar
2 cups white wine vinegar
1 T. pickling spice
1 T. turmeric
4 cloves of garlic
3 T. fresh dill
10 zucchinis, sliced into quarters

BUNS

1 cup whole milk
½ cup water
¼ cup unsalted butter
¼ oz. active dry yeast
4 cups all-purpose flour
1½ T salt
1 T granulated sugar
1 egg
sesame seeds
egg (for egg wash)
Maldon sea salt

BURGERS

ground chuck
(70% lean meat, 30% fat)
cheese

AÏOLI

1 egg yolk
2 t. lemon juice
1 t. garlic, minced
1 t. dijon
1 cup grape seed oil
salt

FRIES

4 quarts frying oil
5 russet potatoes
salt

RECIPE CONTRIBUTED BY

Jacob Town
The Spoon Trade (p. 185)

BREAD AND BUTTER PICKLES

Combine all the ingredients together (except zucchini) in one pot. Bring to a boil until sugar and turmeric have dissolved. Meanwhile, wash the zucchini and slice into quarters (lengthwise), and pack into a canning jar. Once the brining liquid is ready, carefully pour over the zucchini. Let it cool to room temperature and then refrigerate.

BUNS

Preheat oven to 350°F. Warm the milk, water, and butter just enough to melt the butter. Remove from heat and add into a standup mixer. Add the yeast, mix, and let stand for 2 minutes. Add 1 cup of flour to the mixture. Then add the salt and sugar, mix for a few seconds, and add the egg. After the egg is mixed in well, start to add the remaining cups of flour one cup at a time. Scrape down the bowl and mix on low for 7 minutes. Form into eight 4.75 oz. balls and flatten slightly onto a sheet pan lined with parchment paper; cover loosely with plastic wrap, and proof for over 1 hour or until doubled in size. Brush with egg wash and sprinkle with Maldon sea salt. Bake at 350°F for 12 minutes or until golden brown.

BURGERS

Form the raw meat into burger patties of desired weight. On medium-high heat, cook the hamburger patties on one side, then flip once, and cook them on the other side to your preference. Once ready, throw on a slice of your favorite cheese; remove patty from heat once cheese is melted.

AÏOLI

Place yolk, lemon juice, garlic, and dijon in a medium-size mixing bowl. Whisk well to combine. While constantly whisking, start to drizzle a tiny bit of oil into the mixture. Start with a few drops and make sure you are whisking thoroughly. Once you have started to make a strong emulsion, you can add the oil a bit faster. The mixture should start to get thick, like mayonnaise. Once oil is incorporated, add a pinch of salt to taste.

FRIES

Heat the oil in a large pot to 300°F. Meanwhile, cut your potatoes into ¼-inch slices, and put into a water bath. Rinse, drain, and dry potatoes. Place potatoes in the oil and fry for 4 minutes. Remove from oil. Raise the temperature of the oil to 375°F. Fry the potatoes a second time for 5–6 minutes or until crispy. Remove from oil, place on paper towels, and season well with salt. Serve right away.

SANTA MARIA-STYLE TRI-TIP WITH PICO DE GALLO SALSA

The tri-tip, the tri-tip, the tri-tip! That's one thing the locals, current Cal Poly students, university alumni, and tourists can all agree on: SLO has the best tri-tip on the Central Coast. ¡Viva la tri-tip!

TRI-TIP

tri-tip roast
salt
coarsely ground black pepper
granulated garlic

GARLIC BREAD

1 stick salted butter
French or sourdough baguette
garlic salt

PICO DE GALLO SALSA

5 lbs. beefsteak tomatoes
1 whole white onion, finely chopped
1 bunch cilantro, chopped
5 cloves fresh garlic, finely minced
1 whole jalapeño, finely chopped
(more or less to desired heat)
2 limes, juiced (to taste)
1 T salt (to taste)
1 t. pepper
1 t. granulated garlic
½ t. ground cumin
½ t. chili powder
½ t. Mexican oregano

TRI-TIP

Start with an untrimmed tri-tip roast of the highest quality you can find. Trim off all the connective tissue you can see and trim off the fat to ¼-inch thickness across the back of the tri tip. Season generously with salt, coarsely ground black pepper, and granulated garlic.

Grill over medium-high heat, turning every 5–10 minutes, until the internal temperature of the roast is 135°F, usually about 10–15 minutes per pound of meat. Remove from heat and let the tri-tip rest for at least 10 minutes in a shallow pan to catch any juices. Cut the tri-tip across the grain in slices ¼-inch or thinner.

GARLIC BREAD

Place a small pot on the grill and melt a stick of salted butter. Grill a split baguette until crunchy and golden brown. Brush butter on the bread and sprinkle with a small amount of garlic salt.

PICO DE GALLO SALSA

Santa Maria-style tri-tip is most authentically served with fresh *pico de gallo* salsa. Making your own with this easy recipe: Chop tomatoes into a small dice and combine all other ingredients. Mix well.

» Enjoy the tri-tip with hunks of grilled garlic bread and *pico de gallo* salsa served up on a plate or construct a sandwich.

RECIPE CONTRIBUTED BY

Matt Pearce
Old SLO BBQ (p. 172)

WHITE PEACH & OLALLIEBERRY CRUMBLE WITH WHIPPED CREAM

Olallieberries are primarily grown right here on the Central Coast and they have a fleeting season. This unique berry is a special hybrid of a loganberry (blackberry x raspberry) and a youngberry (blackberry x dewberry). Neat, huh?

CRUMBLE FILLING

2 lbs. of firm, ripe peaches
(≈ 6–8 peaches)
2 t. lemon zest
2 T lemon juice, freshly squeezed
½ cup granulated sugar
¼ cup all-purpose flour
1 cup fresh olallieberries (half pint)

CRUMBLE TOPPING

⅔ cup all-purpose flour
⅔ cup brown sugar
⅔ cup oats
4 oz. unsalted butter
salt

WHIPPED CREAM

2 T sugar
1 cup heavy whipping cream
1 t. vanilla extract

Makes 4–6 servings.

CRUMBLE FILLING

Preheat oven to 350°F. Immerse the peaches in boiling water for 30 seconds to 1 minute until the skins can easily be peeled away from the flesh. Immediately place the peaches in cold water. Peel the peaches with a fruit peeler. Once peeled, slice the peaches into thick wedges and place them in a large bowl. Add the lemon zest, lemon juice, sugar, and flour into the bowl. Toss well. Gently mix in the olallieberries. Carefully spoon into individual buttered ramekins.

CRUMBLE TOPPING

In a small bowl, mix the flour, brown sugar, oats, butter, and salt with a fork until it comes together into a crumbly consistency. Sprinkle evenly over the fruit. Place the ramekins onto a sheet pan lined with parchment paper and bake for 40–45 minutes until the top is browned and crisp, and the fruit juices are bubbly.

WHIPPED CREAM

The whipped cream can be made by hand with a whisk, or with a hand mixer with whisk attachment, or with a standup mixer. Regardless of the choice of mixer, the bowl and the utensil (the whisk or whisk attachment) should be placed in the freezer or a very cold refrigerator for 10 minutes before adding the ingredients. Once chilled, add the sugar, whipping cream, and vanilla. Mix on high until the cream reaches stiff peaks.

» Serve warm with a dollop of whipped cream on top.

RECIPE CONTRIBUTED BY

Lisa Schiltz
Meze Wine Bar & Bistro (p. 167)

RASPBERRY LINZER COOKIES

These cookies are easy as 1, 2, 3. They are extremely versatile in that you can make them year-round; just substitute your favorite seasonal jam if raspberries aren't available.

COOKIES

1 lb. unsalted butter, chilled
1 cup plus 1 T granulated sugar
¼ t. salt
1 T vanilla
2 eggs
5½ cups all-purpose flour
powdered sugar

RASPBERRY JAM

8 oz. basket of raspberries
8 oz. sugar
1 T lemon juice

COOKIES

Chop the butter into small cubes and add to a standup mixer with a paddle attachment. Add sugar and salt; mix until smooth—some small chunks are okay. Add vanilla. Add eggs one at a time and mix until incorporated. Scrape the sides of the bowl. Add flour slowly and mix on low until dough comes together and flour is incorporated. Place dough on a parchment-covered sheet pan. Place another piece of parchment on top of the dough and press the dough out until it's somewhat flat. Chill in the refrigerator for 20–30 minutes. Preheat oven to 350°F. Remove dough from fridge and lightly dust the surface with flour to keep the rolling pin from sticking. Roll the dough to ¼-inch thickness and use a cookie cutter to cut out your cookies. If you'd like to go for the Linzer look, punch a hole in half of the batch. Bake for 10–12 minutes or until golden. Let cookies cool on a rack before assembling.

RASPBERRY JAM

Place raspberries, sugar, and lemon juice in a large copper pot. Bring to a boil over medium heat, stirring until sugar is dissolved. Simmer over low heat, stir occasionally for 25–30 min until thick. Place a saucer in the freezer to chill, then test the thickness of the jam by placing a spoonful onto the cold saucer. Run your finger through the jam. If the line remains, then it's thick enough. Carefully pour the jam into a glass container and let it cool.

Don't feel like doing the extra step of making raspberry jam from scratch? Pick up a jar of your favorite fruit preserves from Lori of Mama's Preserves (p. 166) at the downtown Thursday night market!

» Lightly dust only the cookies with holes with sifted powdered sugar. Assemble the cookies—sandwich together with a heaping tablespoon of jam in the middle with the hole-side up.

RECIPE CONTRIBUTED BY

Jeremy Davenport
Éclair Bakery (p. 156)

ZABAGLIONE

The Marsala wine adds significant depth to this simple Italian custard dessert. Serve alongside fresh seasonal berries, whipped cream, and biscotti. Buon appetito!

ZABAGLIONE

6 egg yolks
⅓ cup granulated sugar
1 t. grated lemon peel
pinch of ground cinnamon
drop of vanilla extract
¾ cup sweet Marsala wine
1 cup heavy cream
berries and/or biscotti

Yields 6 servings.

ZABAGLIONE

Place egg yolks and sugar in a large, round-bottomed stainless steel bowl. Add grated lemon peel, a pinch of cinnamon, and a drop of vanilla extract to the yolk mixture. Pour in the sweet Marsala wine. Tip: You can use sweet Vermouth as a substitute for the Marsala.

Fill a pot halfway with water, bring the water to a simmer, then reduce the heat to low. Set the bowl containing the custard mixture over the simmering water; the bottom of the bowl should not touch the water. Whisk the custard mixture, making sure that the water does not boil. This ensures that a gentle, even heat thickens the mixture without curdling it. Whisking traps air in the yolks for a light, fluffy mixture.

Continue whisking for about 10 minutes, until the mixture triples in volume, froths up, and becomes pale. When it reaches this desired consistency, take the bowl of custard off of the pot. Longer cooking will thicken the custard further, giving it the texture of mousse. Continue whisking for a minute or two to prevent the custard from sticking to the bowl.

Set aside the custard for about 15 minutes to cool. In a standup mixer, whisk heavy cream until it forms soft peaks; add the whipped heavy cream to the cooled custard, using a whisk to gently fold them together. Reserve some of the whipped cream to serve on top. Ladle the zabaglione into individual dishes. Serve with whipped cream, berries, and/or biscotti.

RECIPE CONTRIBUTED BY
Nicola Allegretta
Mama's Meatball (p. 165)

AUTUMN

PUMPKIN WAFFLES WITH CARDAMOM CREAM & BROWN BUTTER SYRUP

You know it's officially fall when these pumpkin waffles re-appear on the menu at Sally Loo's. They are doused in brown butter syrup, cardamom mascarpone cream, and topped with locally grown apples, and toasted pecans. Yup, autumn is here!

PUMPKIN WAFFLE BATTER

5 lb. pumpkin (8 oz. pumpkin purée)
2 cups all-purpose flour
2 T. sugar
½ t. baking soda
2 t. baking powder
½ t. salt
1 t. cinnamon
pinch of cloves
pinch of allspice
pinch of ginger
pinch of nutmeg, freshly grated
1 egg
3 T. butter, melted
2 cups buttermilk
zest of an orange

BROWN BUTTER SYRUP

2 sticks butter
½ cup hot water
1 cup brown sugar

CARDAMOM MASCARPONE CREAM

8 oz. mascarpone cheese
1 cup heavy cream
¾ cup powdered sugar
pinch of cardamom
1 t. vanilla extract

GARNISH

apple slices
toasted pecans

RECIPE CONTRIBUTED BY

Jen Manuele
Sally Loo's (p. 181)

PUMPKIN WAFFLE BATTER

You can make your own pumpkin purée by roasting, scooping, and puréeing a whole pumpkin. Preheat oven to 350°F. Remove the stem, cut the pumpkin in half, and scoop out the seeds. Place the pumpkin cut-side down on a parchment-lined baking sheet. Bake for about 45 minutes until the pumpkin's flesh is easily pierced with a fork. Remove it from the oven, scoop out the flesh, and purée it using a food processor or by simply mashing it.

Mix your dry ingredients together in a big bowl: flour, sugar, baking soda, baking powder, salt, cinnamon, cloves, allspice, ginger, and nutmeg.

In a separate bowl, whisk egg yolk into soft peaks (whisk the egg white into soft peaks separately and set aside for later). Add whisked egg yolk to the dry ingredients. Add the melted butter, buttermilk, pumpkin purée, and orange zest. Fold in whisked egg white.

Heat up your waffle iron and pour accordingly. The recipe makes approximately 12 waffles, depending on the size of your iron.

BROWN BUTTER SYRUP

Brown the butter in a saucepan. In a separate pot, heat the water and sugar together to form a simple syrup. Once the sugar is completely dissolved, mix in the melted butter. Bada bing!

CARDAMOM MASCARPONE CREAM

In a standup mixer, whip together the mascarpone cheese and the heavy cream. Add in the powdered sugar, cardamom, and vanilla. Mix on high until it forms stiff peaks.

GARNISH

Garnish your waffle with sliced apples, toasted pecans, a generous dollop of cardamom mascarpone cream, and a drizzling of the brown butter syrup.

RYE PANCAKES WITH APPLE COMPOTE & WALNUT GRANOLA

On a crisp autumn morning these rye pancakes will make you leap out of your cozy bed to make brunch. Complete with caramelized apple compote, cardamom chantilly, and crunchy walnut granola!

RYE PANCAKES

1 ¼ cups all-purpose flour
1 cup rye flour
2 t. baking powder
1 t. baking soda
¾ t. salt
2 eggs
3 cups buttermilk
5 T melted butter

CARAMELIZED APPLE COMPOTE

2 Fuji apples
½ cup orange juice, fresh squeezed
1 T lemon juice, fresh squeezed
½ t. minced ginger
1 t. orange zest
⅛ t. mace
¼ cup brown sugar
pinch of salt

CARDAMOM CHANTILLY

1 t. cardamom powder
1 pinch cinnamon
2 T powdered sugar
1 cup heavy whipping cream
1 t. vanilla

WALNUT GRANOLA

1 ½ cups of agave syrup
¼ cup olive oil
4 cups oats
4½ cups raw walnuts
½ t. salt

RECIPE CONTRIBUTED BY

Shanny Covey
Robin's Restaurant (p.178)

RYE PANCAKES

Place all ingredients in a bowl and mix until smooth. Let rest 15 minutes before using the batter. Place a skillet on medium heat. Once heated, butter the surface. With a measuring cup, pour ½ cup of batter to make uniform pancakes. It will take a couple of minutes per side. Once little bubbles appear on the surface, take a peek to see if the bottom is golden brown, then flip to cook the other side. Serve immediately or pop them on a baking tray in the oven at 200°F to keep the batch warm. Between batches, wipe down the cooking surface with a paper napkin and add more butter as needed.

CARAMELIZED APPLE COMPOTE

Peel and core apples. Cut into ¼-inch cubes. Add the apples and the rest of ingredients to a medium sauce pan. Simmer for 8–10 minutes or until the apples are tender and the liquid has reduced to a medium syrup.

CARDAMOM CHANTILLY

Place all ingredients in a standup mixer. Mix on high until it forms stiff peaks.

WALNUT GRANOLA

Mix all ingredients together. Bake for 30 minutes at 350°F. After 15 minutes, remove from heat. Stir mixture with a spatula, rotate the orientation of the pan, and place back into the oven until golden brown.

» Stack up your pancakes, load them up with caramelized apple compote and walnut granola, and top it all off with some cardamom chantilly. Enjoy!

YOGURT WITH MACERATED SEASONAL FRUIT

I like to macerate fruit in a bowl with a bit of sugar, store it overnight, and put it in my yogurt the following morning. It's a fun way to transform an otherwise plain yogurt flavor into a super juicy, fruity flavor!

YOGURT

your favorite berries or stone fruit
granulated sugar
half a lemon, juiced
your favorite yogurt
your favorite nuts, chopped
your favorite honey

YOGURT

Thoroughly wash and dry fruit. Small berries like raspberries, blackberries, blueberries, olallieberries, and boysenberries can be kept whole, but if using larger fruits, like peaches, nectarines, or strawberriesberries, cut them into bite-size pieces.

Once the fruit is prepped, place in a glass container. Sprinkle a few large spoonfuls of sugar over the berries. Sugar will draw the moisture out of the fruit, which will then combine with the sugar in the bowl and will result in a delicious fruit syrup. Squeeze half a lemon over the berries, close the container, and shake so everything is evenly coated.

Let the fruit sit at room temperature for 30 minutes to start the macerating process, then place the container in the refrigerator until serving. The longer you let the fruit mascerate, the longer the fruit has to break down and steep in its own sugars. Serve the morning after or the following day.

» In a bowl, combine your yogurt, heaping spoonfuls of the macerated fruit, chopped nuts, and a drizzle of honey.

Experiment with using your favorite liqueurs, vinegars, sweeteners (honey, maple syrup, agave), spices, fresh herbs, and extracts (vanilla, almond). One of my personal favorite flavor combinations is strawberries with balsamic vinegar and black pepper!

RECIPE CREATED BY
Kendra Aronson (p. 6)

NAPA CABBAGE WRAPS WITH ROASTED PEPPERS & CHICKEN

This makes for a great party platter: roasted bell peppers, onions, and chicken; queso fresco, cilantro, topped with a creamy, spicy adobo sauce and wrapped up in the perfect edible vessel—Napa cabbage.

WRAPS

1 red bell pepper
1 orange bell pepper
1 large sweet onion
3 T olive oil
salt and pepper
1 head of Napa Cabbage
(from Talley Farms, p. 187)
shredded roasted chicken
queso fresco
cilantro

CRÈME FRAÎCHE ADOBO SAUCE

5 oz. crème fraîche
5 oz. can chipotle peppers in adobo sauce

WRAPS

Preheat oven to 350°F. Slice the tops off of the peppers and cut in half, taking out the core and seeds. Cut the sweet onion into slices. Toss the peppers and onions with olive oil, salt, and pepper; roast in the oven until the vegetables start to caramelize (approximately 35–45 minutes). Remove from the oven.

While the peppers and onions are cooling, wash the Napa cabbage. Use the smaller inner leaves to make small wraps; you will have plenty of leftover cabbage to use for another recipe, e.g., a stir fry. When peppers are cool enough to handle, slice into thin strips.

CRÈME FRAÎCHE ADOBO SAUCE

With a mini food processor, blend together the crème fraîche, one tablespoon of the adobo sauce, and one chipotle pepper from the can. Put the mixture into a squeeze bottle.

» Lay out the cabbage leaves on a platter. Assemble each wrap to your liking: top with the mixture of peppers and onions, shredded roasted chicken (p. 68), queso fresco, and cilantro. Finish with a drizzle of the spicy crème fraîche adobo sauce.

RECIPE CREATED BY
Sarah Matthews
Talley Farms (p. 187)

GARLICKY BLACKENED BRUSSELS SPROUTS WITH MEYER LEMON AÏOLI

These Brussels sprouts sure do pack a punch! Between the garlicky aïoli, vibrant lemon juice, and salty bacon, you will always have a hankering to make this easy comfort dish.

BRUSSELS SPROUTS

1 T olive oil
1 lb. Brussels sprouts (similar size)
(from Pepper Creek Family Farms, p. 174)
3-4 strips of bacon, chopped
1 Meyer lemon
splash of white wine (≈ ¼ cup)
5-6 cloves of garlic, minced

AÏOLI

soft butter
mayonnaise
Meyer lemon juice
garlic salt
garlic cloves

BRUSSELS SPROUTS

Clean, trim, and wash the Brussels sprouts. Cut them in half—this way the garlic and lemon juice can get into all the folds. Steam for 5–7 minutes so they cook halfway through. Next, heat up a skillet to medium heat, and drizzle olive oil twice around the skillet. Add the steamed Brussels and raw chopped bacon. With one half of the Meyer lemon, slice into thin coins, remove the seeds, and add the slices to the skillet. With the other half of the lemon, squeeze the juice all around the skillet coating the Brussels sprouts and bacon.

It takes around 10 minutes for the Brussels and lemons to caramelize. When they are a deep, dark caramelized brown and the skillet has all that good stuff sticking to it, add a couple splashes of white wine to deglaze the skillet. Add the garlic. Only sauté for 1–2 minutes to avoid burning the garlic. Plate and serve with aïoli.

AÏOLI

In a food processor, combine equal parts of soft butter and mayo—make as much as you'd like. Add the juice from half of a Meyer lemon, add a couple dashes of garlic salt, and a couple cloves of garlic. Pulse a few times, season to taste, and serve on the side.

RECIPE CONTRIBUTED BY
Jessica Newell
Pepper Creek Family Farms (p. 174)

SWEET YAMS WITH BROWN SUGAR PECAN CRUMBLE

This dish may steal the Thanksgiving show—it is so sweet, creamy, buttery, and irresistibly tasty. Making a double batch is advisable since it's highly likely you'll be going back for seconds (or thirds)!

SWEET YAMS

3 medium yams, mashed
1 cup brown sugar
3 eggs
¾ cup whole milk
¼ cup half-and-half
1 stick butter, melted
1 t. vanilla

BROWN SUGAR PECAN CRUMBLE

1 cup pecans, chopped
½ c. flour
1 cup brown sugar
1 stick of butter, melted

SWEET YAMS

Tip from Tami Righetti (p. 176): "I bake the yams instead of boiling them so that they have a richer, more robust flavor." Preheat oven to 425°F. Bake sweet yams on a cookie sheet for 40–60 minutes. After 30 minutes, check on the yams. Once they are soft enough, you should be able to poke/puncture them with a fork. Remove yams from the oven. Lower the oven temperature to 350°F.

Once the yams are cool enough to handle, place 1 yam inside a kitchen towel, gently roll to soften flesh. Unwrap the towel, cut an "X" at the top of the yam, and push the flesh forward into a bowl. Repeat for the remaining yams. Mash with a hand mixer until smooth.

Next, add the sugar, eggs, milk, half-and-half, melted butter, and vanilla. Mix until smooth. Pour mixture into a large buttered casserole dish.

BROWN SUGAR PECAN CRUMBLE

Mix pecans, flour, brown sugar, and melted butter together in a bowl with your hands. Once it reaches a crumbly consistency, crumble over the yams.

» Bake for 30–35 minutes at 350°F. Wiggle the casserole dish, the yams should be a pudding-like consistency when done. Remove from the oven. Let sit for 5 minutes before serving.

RECIPE CONTRIBUTED BY

Tami Righetti
Righetti Ranch (p. 176)

BUTTERNUT SQUASH & GREEN APPLE SOUP

I love this unique pairing of earthy butternut squash with tart green apple. Drizzle on some crème fraîche, garnish with chopped chives, and finish with a generous amount of freshly cracked pepper on this autumn soup.

SOUP

1 T. butter
1 yellow onion, diced
1 rib of celery, diced
1 carrot, diced
1 large butternut squash
(≈ 6 cups chopped)
(from Esther's Garden, p. 158)
1–2 tart green apples
(≈ 2 cups chopped)
3 cups of chicken or veggie broth
pinch of nutmeg
salt and pepper

GARNISH

crème fraîche
chives, chopped
pepper

Yields 4–6 servings.

SOUP

Combine butter, onion, celery, and carrot in large saucepan over medium heat. Cook for 5 minutes. While this *mirepoix* is cooking, prep the squash and apples. Peel, remove seeds, and chop the butternut squash. Peel, core, and chop the apples. The squash to apple ratio should be 3:1.

Add the chopped squash, chopped apple, and broth to the *mirepoix*. Bring to a boil. Simmer for 10 minutes or until squash is soft. Purée with a handmixer. Add spices to taste.

GARNISH

In a squeeze bottle, add some crème fraîche. Thin out the crème fraîche with a splash of milk if needed. Drizzle in a circular motion over the top of each bowl of soup; garnish with chopped chives and freshly cracked pepper. Serve with a nice slab of crusty, buttery bread (p. 162).

RECIPE CONTRIBUTED BY
Esther Rigoni
Esther's Garden (p. 158)

ROASTED BEET & BLUE CHEESE SALAD WITH SHERRY VINAIGRETTE

This hearty salad can stand on its own as a satisfying meal: colorful roasted beets, freshly picked greens, creamy blue cheese, crunchy almonds—all tossed together with a vibrant vinaigrette.

SALAD

4 medium red beets
4 medium golden beets
3 T olive oil
3 T sherry vinegar
salt and pepper
2 cups mixed greens
¼ cup Marcona almonds, roasted and salted
4 oz. Gorgonzola cheese, crumbled

SALAD

Preheat oven to 400°F. Wash, trim, and scrub the beets. Wrap beets individually in foil—enclosing completely—and place them on a sheet pan. Roast them for 50 minutes to 1 hour until tender (easily pierced with a fork). Unwrap the beets and set aside until cool enough to handle. Peel beets with a paring knife. Cut the beets into wedges.

Whisk together the olive oil and vinegar in a small bowl. Season to taste with salt and pepper. Set aside.

Place the mixed greens in a bowl, drizzle with vinaigrette. Toss gently to evenly coat the greens. Arrange the greens on individual plates or in a big serving bowl.

» Arrange the beets on top of the greens; top with the almonds and cheese.

RECIPE CONTRIBUTED BY
Lisa Schiltz
Meze Wine Bar & Bistro (p. 167)

BUTTERNUT SQUASH, GOAT CHEESE, & HAZELNUT GRATIN

I suggest preparing this gratin casserole the night before Thanksgiving. Once you are getting close to turkey time, bake it off with the cream and hazelnuts. Then garnish with sage leaves before serving.

GRATIN

3 lbs. Butternut squash, peeled, seeded, and cubed
4 T olive oil
salt and pepper
4 medium leeks, sliced
6 oz. fresh chèvre
1 cup heavy cream
¾ cup toasted hazelnuts, chopped
1 T fresh sage leaves, chopped

GRATIN

Preheat oven to 400°F. Toss the cubed squash with two tablespoons of olive oil; season with salt and pepper. Spread out on a baking sheet, roast for 30–40 minutes until starting to brown.

Slice the leeks up to the tough, dark green parts. Submerge in water and drain to remove all the dirt. Sauté the leeks with the remaining olive oil until thoroughly wilted. Remove from heat.

Butter a suitable casserole dish and layer the dish with leeks first, squash next, and then chèvre. Repeat until all the ingredients are used up. You can refrigerate this casserole at this point for later use—otherwise, pour the cream over the whole casserole and top with chopped hazelnuts.

Bake at 400°F until the cream is bubbling; start checking after 30 minutes. Top with fresh sage leaves before serving.

RECIPE CONTRIBUTED BY
Greg Holt
Big Sky Cafe (p. 152)

ROASTED CHICKEN

"If there was ever a single ingredient that I felt deserved a consistent spot on our menu, it was local chicken. Chicken is cheap, underappreciated, and underutilized by most Americans. People assume it can't be spectacular. Game on!"

CHICKEN

whole chicken
salt
buttermilk
water
8 oz. unsalted butter
8 oz. canola

CHICKEN

Make a brine based on the weight of the whole chicken with the following ratios: 2% kosher salt, 2% buttermilk, 96% water. Submerge the whole chicken in the brine; refrigerate for 24 hours. Once brined, allow chicken to air-dry in the refrigerator for 1–2 days on a wire rack.

Preheat oven to 475°F. Place the chicken on a wire rack in a roasting pan. Roast for 40 minutes, basting and rotating every 20 minutes. Tip from Chef Jensen (p. 154): "The quantity of the baste is pretty arbitrary. You just need enough to baste the chicken a few times, the drippings from the chicken will also add to the amount, use approximately 8 ounces of melted butter and 8 ounces of canola. Basically you are just making a butter-based baste with the heat resilience of canola. This keeps the butter solids from burning too quickly, without having to clarify the butter, plus the little bits of caramelized fat solids from the butter are tasty!"

Reduce oven temperature to 350°F and finish roasting, approximately 20–30 minutes. The probe thermometer should read 145–150°F at the thickest part of the breast. Allow chicken to rest in a warm area for at least a half hour prior to portioning.

RECIPE CONTRIBUTED BY
Chef Jensen Lorenzen
Formerly of The Cass House
Inn & Restaurant (p. 154)

SHEA'S LEFTOVER THANKSGIVING TURKEY SOUP

Enjoy another meal of gobble, gobble goodness. "Proportions are suggestions in keeping with the Thanksgiving leftovers vibe. I like cutting the veggies in a rough chop rather than a precise dice."—Shea Somma, Master Turkey Fryer of the Universe.

TURKEY BROTH

leftover Thanksgiving turkey carcass

TURKEY SOUP

4 T butter
1 yellow onion, chopped
1 bunch celery, chopped
1 bunch carrots, chopped
1 t. salt
1½ cup of wild rice
14 cups turkey broth
3 cups leftover turkey, chopped
salt and pepper

TURKEY BROTH

Don't let your Thanksgiving turkey carcass go to waste! You can make a delicious stock that can be refrigerated for up to a week or frozen for up to 6 months. In a large stock pot, add the carcass—you may need to break up the bones in order to fit it inside the pot. Cover with water, making sure that everything is submerged. Bring to a boil over high heat. Reduce to low and simmer. Skim fat occasionally during the simmering process with a ladle. Simmer for 2–3 hours until the turkey flavor comes through, strain through a mesh strainer. Let cool to room temperature then refrigerate or freeze.

TURKEY SOUP

On medium heat, melt two tablespoons of butter in a stock pot. Add the *mirepoix* (onion, celery, and carrots) to the pot; stir occasionally. Once the vegetables start to sizzle, turn down the heat, add salt, and let the vegetables sweat and soften.

Add the remaining butter, then add the rice. Mix the rice thoroughly—you want the rice to be coated in butter. Keep stirring frequently so the rice does not burn, you will start to smell the rice toasting. Once the rice gives off a strong toasted scent, you are ready to add the broth.

Add approximately 14 cups of your homemade turkey broth to the pot. Turn up the heat, bring to a boil, then back down to a simmer once it starts to boil. Skim the fat with a ladle. Chop the leftover turkey into bite-size pieces and mince turkey skins into little bits, yielding approximately 3 cups. Add the turkey to the soup; salt and pepper to taste. Serve immediately.

RECIPE CONTRIBUTED BY

Shea Somma (p. 3) a.k.a.
Kendra Aronson's squeeze!

TURKISH SPICED LAMB WITH SALTY JAJIK

"Turkey was the first place I ever had sheep's milk yogurt—that was back in the 60s!" reminisces cheesemaker Christine Maguire of Rinconada Dairy. You will love this comforting Turkish lamb dish with salty jajik.

RICE

- 2 cups basmati rice
- 1 onion, minced
- 1½ t. cinnamon
- 1 t. whole coriander seeds
- ¼ cup currants
- ¼ cup golden raisins

LAMB

- 2 T. ghee
- 1 onion, chopped
- 1 lb. lamb shoulder, cubed
- 1 t. whole coriander seeds
- 2 cloves of garlic, chopped
- 28 oz. canned tomatoes, crushed
- 1–3 T. cinnamon
- 1–2 t. allspice
- 1–2 t. thyme
- ¼ cup pine nuts, toasted
- ½ cup parsley, chopped
- ½ cup almonds, sliced

JAJIK

- 2 cups sheep's milk yogurt (from Rinconada Dairy, p. 177)
- 1 cucumber, peeled, seeded, grated
- 2 cloves of garlic, chopped
- salt and pepper

Yields 4 servings.

RICE

Prepare the basmati rice. While the rice is cooking, stir fry the onion with the cinnamon, remove from the heat. Once the rice is steamed, add it to the onion pan along with the whole coriander seeds, currants, and golden raisins. Mix well to incorporate all the ingredients and spices.

LAMB

Heat up a cast-iron skillet over medium-high heat. Once hot, add the ghee, onion, and lamb. Sauté gently while mixing in the coriander seeds and garlic. Once the meat starts to brown, add in the tomatoes and cinnamon. Stir everything, the lamb should be completely coated. The meat will continue to brown and the mixture will start to thicken up a bit. Add in the allspice and thyme, then adjust the heat to low. In a separate pan, toast the pine nuts and set aside.

JAJIK

Optional: drain the sheep's milk yogurt for a thicker *jajik*. Squeeze the liquid out of the grated cucumber. Add the cucumber and garlic to the yogurt, stir well. Add a lot of salt—you want the *jajik* to taste salty. Season with pepper to taste.

» Plate the rice on a platter, place the meat on top of the rice. Garnish generously with pine nuts, parsley, and almonds. Serve with *jajik* on the side.

RECIPE CONTRIBUTED BY

Christine Maguire
Rinconada Dairy (p. 177)

SHEEP'S MILK VANILLA ICE CREAM WITH GRILLED FIGS

I'm a huge fan of this local sheep's milk ice cream—in fact we had Negranti's adorable ice cream truck at our wedding! I love to pair her vanilla flavor with grilled figs and a savory drizzle of balsamic vinegar and olive oil.

ICE CREAM
figs
olive oil
balsamic vinegar
granulated sugar
vanilla sheep's milk ice cream
(from Negranti Creamery, p. 169)

ICE CREAM

Cut the stems off each fig and cut in half lengthwise. In a bowl, whisk together equal ratios of olive oil, balsamic vinegar, and sugar to evenly coat the quantity of figs you have. Add the figs to the bowl, toss very gently (figs are very fragile) to evenly coat.

Fire up your grill—if necessary, brush a little olive oil to your grill to avoid sticking. Grill the figs cut-side down so they rest evenly. With tongs, check the figs after 2–3 minutes. Once the grill marks appear on the flesh, remove from heat—do not overcook the figs as they will turn out mushy.

Scoop ice cream servings into individual bowls. Top with grilled figs, and a drizzle of olive oil and balsamic vinegar to your liking.

RECIPE CREATED BY
Kendra Aronson (p. 6)

APPLE TARTLET WITH BUTTERY BROWN SUGAR STREUSEL

This crust is the same dough recipe used to make Raspberry Linzer Cookies (p. 44). This beautiful apple tartlet with its flaky, buttery, golden crust and crumbly streusel will make your heart sing.

CRUST

1 lb. unsalted butter, chilled
1 cup plus 1 T granulated sugar
¼ t. salt
1 T vanilla
2 eggs
5½ cups all-purpose flour

FILLING

1 T butter
2 t. water
4 green apples, cored, peeled, and cubed
¼ cup granulated sugar
½ T lemon juice
¼ t. cinnamon

STREUSEL

1 cup oats
2 cups all-purpose flour
1 cup brown sugar
4 oz. butter, melted
1 T vanilla extract

CRUST

Preheat oven to 350°F. Chop the butter into small cubes and add to a standup mixer with a paddle attachment. Add sugar and salt; mix until smooth—some small chunks are okay. Add vanilla. Add eggs one at a time and mix until incorporated. Scrape the sides of the bowl. Add flour slowly, mix on low until dough comes together and flour is incorporated.

Place dough on a parchment paper covered sheet pan. Place another piece of paper on top of the dough and press the dough out until it's somewhat flat. Chill in the fridge for 20–30 minutes.

Remove dough from fridge and lightly dust the surface with flour to keep the rolling pin from sticking. Roll the dough to ¼-inch thickness and to the desired diameter of your tartlet pans. Transfer the dough to the bottom and the sides of the pan. Pierce a few times with a fork—this will release any heat pressure during baking. Bake for 10–12 minutes or until golden.

FILLING

Place butter, water, and apples in a pan on medium heat for 5–7 minutes shaking the pan occasionally to move the apples around. Once they're tender, remove pan from the heat. Drain and cool completely. Stir in sugar, lemon juice, and cinnamon.

STREUSEL

Incorporate all the ingredients together in a bowl, mix by hand. It is done when you are able to squeeze a bit in your hand and it holds its shape.

» Fill the par-baked tartlets with the apple mixture and top with a generous amount of streusel on top. Bake at 350°F for 10 minutes or until the streusel is golden.

RECIPE CONTRIBUTED BY
Jeremy Davenport
Éclair Bakery (p. 156)

PISTACHIO CRUST HONEYED GOAT CHEESE CHEESECAKE

This unique cheesecake is a real treat—tangy goat cheese, citrusy crème, buttery pistachio crust, pillowy whipped cream, and sweet local honey. It's a little time intensive, but totally worthwhile and super delicious.

PISTACHIO CRUST

1 heaping cup pistachios, toasted
½ cup brown sugar
3 T butter, melted

FILLING

2 lbs. fresh goat cheese
⅔ cup granulated sugar
1 ¼ cups Mascarpone cheese
2 oz. honey
½ t. vanilla extract
½ t. salt
8 eggs

CITRUS CRÈME

4 oz. butter, room temperature
½ cup granulated sugar
2 eggs
2 egg yolks
2 t. citrus zest (lemon, lime, or orange)
¼ cup orange juice
¼ cup lemon juice
1 oz. lime juice
¼ t. vanilla extract
1 pinch salt
1 cup heavy cream

GARNISH

whipped cream
pistachios, chopped
local honey

PISTACHIO CRUST

Preheat oven to 350°F. In a food processor, pulse pistachios and brown sugar until it resembles sand. Do not over pulse or you will make pistachio butter. Add in the melted butter and pulse until the mixture resembles wet sand.

Fill the bottom of a 9-inch cake pan with the crust, bake for 10 minutes. Do not let the crust brown. Let cool before you add the filling.

FILLING

Lower oven to 325°F. Make sure both the goat cheese and Mascarpone cheese are at room temperature. Blend all ingredients (in the order they are listed) in a standup mixer on high, whip until fluffy.

Pour the filling into the par-baked crust. Bake for 45–60 minutes until the cheesecake is set—just jiggly. Do not let it brown or crack. Remove from the oven, let rest until it reaches room temperature. Refrigerate for a few hours.

CITRUS CRÈME

Whisk butter and sugar together until pale yellow and fluffy. Slowly add in eggs and egg yolks until fully incorporated. Add in zest, citrus juices, vanilla, and salt. Over a double boiler, whisk mixture and bring to 165°F (or until it coats the back of a spoon). Strain mixture into a bowl and slowly whisk in heavy cream. Refrigerate to cool.

GARNISH

Remove the cheesecake and bowl of crème from the refrigerator. With a spatula, distribute the crème evenly over the cheesecake. Garnish with whipped cream, chopped pistachios, and local honey.

RECIPE CONTRIBUTED BY

Shaun Behrens
Luna Red Restaurant•Bar (p. 164)

WINTER

PISTACHIO SHORTBREAD COOKIES WITH LEMON GLAZE

"Shortbread cookies are so easy and can be changed seasonally, so this recipe can be used as a springboard to try lots of flavor combinations. Lemon pistachio was a late winter addition to our menu and it has become a favorite!"

SHORTBREAD
2 sticks butter, room temperature
½ cup cane sugar
1 t. salt
1 t. vanilla paste
zest of 1 lemon
2 cups all-purpose flour
½ cup ground pistachios

GLAZE
2 cups powdered sugar
⅓ cup lemon juice, fresh squeezed
2 T lemon zest
ground pistachios

SHORTBREAD

"Because this recipe is so minimal on the ingredients, you need to use the best you can find," suggests Sara, Baker/Owner of Scout Coffee Co. (p. 182).

In a standup mixer, cream the butter. Add sugar and continue mixing until pillowy and fluffy. Add salt, vanilla paste, and lemon zest; mix for 30 seconds. Combine flour and ground pistachios in a small bowl. Mix into the standup mixer in 2 additions until just combined—don't overmix. Turn shortbread dough out onto a work surface, pat it into a disk, wrap and place in fridge to chill for 30 minutes to an hour.

Preheat oven to 325°F. Lightly flour work surface. Cover dough in parchment paper to make rolling out easier. Roll the dough out to your liking: ¼-inch thickness will result in crispy cookies, ½-inch thickness will result in thicker cookies. Cut shortbread using a cookie cutter of your choice. Place on parchment-lined sheet pans. Bake for approximately 22 minutes.

GLAZE

Add powdered sugar to a bowl, whisk in lemon juice and lemon zest until smooth. Use an offset spatula to spread glaze, sprinkle with pistachios, and let sit for a few minutes to set.

RECIPE CONTRIBUTED BY
Sara Peterson
Scout Coffee Co. (p. 182)

GRILLED SAUSAGE, EGGS, HASSELBLAD POTATOES, & PESTO

Hunker down with this hefty breakfast of champions: grilled sausage, farm fresh eggs, visually-striking Hasselblad potatoes, and a dangerously delicious pesto.

POTATOES, SAUSAGE, & EGGS

fingerling potatoes
olive oil
butter
salt and pepper
raw sausage links
(from Cal Poly, p. 153)
eggs

SPICY PISTACHIO PESTO

⅓ cup spicy roasted pistachios
⅓ cup hard sheep's milk cheese
(from Rinconada Dairy, p. 177)
2 cups fresh basil leaves
(from SLO Grown Produce, p. 184)
5 cloves of garlic
red pepper flakes
½ cup olive oil
(from Lone Oak Olive Oil, p. 184)
salt and pepper

POTATOES, SAUSAGE, & EGGS

Preheat oven to 425°F. To achieve potatoes that are crispy on the outside yet tender on the inside (a winning combo!) try the Hasselblad method. Cut slits in each potato while still maintaining a connection at the bottom. Place into a cast-iron skillet, drizzle with olive oil and dabs of butter, season with salt and pepper. Roast in the oven for 35–45 minutes until crispy and tender.

For the sausage, cook over medium-high heat in a grill pan until browned, about 5 minutes, turning links often. Cover for 12 minutes or until cooked through. Prepare the eggs to your liking: poached, fried, sunny side up, etc.

SPICY PISTACHIO PESTO

In a food processor, combine the pistachios, cheese, basil, garlic, and red pepper flakes. Pulse until combined into a paste. Blend together and slowly drizzle in oil as it forms into a smooth sauce. Taste for seasoning and spiciness level; adjust accordingly with salt, pepper, and red pepper flakes.

» Plate the potatoes, sausage, and egg. Douse with pesto and chow down.

RECIPE CREATED BY
Kendra Aronson (p. 6)

JULIA'S JUICE BLENDS

These are not exact recipes—rather these are some juice blends and flavor combinations provided by Julia. May they inspire you to start your very own at-home juicing experiments!

NOPAL AND SPINACH

nopal (cactus)
spinach
parsley
celery
grapefruit

TROPIC FUSION

carrot
apple
mango

GINGY BEET

orange
carrot
beet
ginger

GREEN VEGGIE BLAST

kale
fennel
arugula
carrot
apple

CAYENNE BEET

cilantro
ginger
cayenne
beet
celery
apple

JULIA'S JUICES

"Julia's Juices (p. 161) offers high-quality juices. Aside from farming most of our own pesticide-free produce, we use a high-end press that extracts all nutrients, enzymes, acids, proteins, and soluble fibers so that your body receives the maximum nutrients. The Norwalk extractor was invented by a doctor who believes in the power of naturally derived raw nutrients. Raw cold-pressed juices provide your body with instant nutrition, all nutrients are absorbed into the bloodstream within 15 minutes of ingestion and gives you a boost of energy and a high sense of alertness. Raw juices are also very effective in naturally detoxing and cleansing your entire system, from your blood to your digestive system, and help to stabilize your entire body." Below she describes the flavor profiles of her popular juice combinations:

NOPAL AND SPINACH

Mild green, herbaceous, and slightly briny with a light sweetness.

TROPIC FUSION

Slightly earthy, rich, and sweet with a tropical twist of fruit.

GINGY BEET

Earthy, sweet, and citrusy with a slight spice from the ginger.

GREEN VEGGIE BLAST

Light green flavor, licoricey, sweet with a nice herbal spice.

CAYENNE BEET

Spicy, sweet, briny, herbal, and earthy.

RECIPE CONTRIBUTED BY
Julia Gomez
Julia's Juices (p. 161)

MUSHROOM & LEEK QUICHE

This buttery, flaky, cheesy vegetable quiche is a great breakfast, mid-morning snack, or light lunch. For a more complete meal, serve alongside mixed greens tossed with your favorite vinaigrette.

CRUST

1 cup of unbleached flour
¼ cup whole wheat flour
¼ t. salt
1 stick of cold butter
3 T cold water

FILLING

4 T butter
3 cups leeks, sliced
3 cups mushrooms, sliced
6 eggs
1 T garlic, finely minced
3 t. grated ginger
1 T unbleached flour
2¼ cups half-and-half
salt and pepper
1 cup grated Parmesan

CRUST

Mix the flours and salt in a food processor. Cut in the cold butter. Slowly add the cold water by pulsing until the dough forms a ball. Form the dough into a disc; cover in plastic wrap and chill for 1 hour.

Preheat oven to 400°F. On a floured surface, roll out dough until it covers the bottom and sides of a 7-inch round deep pie dish. Roll the dough onto the rolling pin and unroll it over the dish. Press the dough lightly into the bottom of the dish, trim the excess dough off. Prick the bottom on the dough with a fork in ½-inch intervals. Place a piece of parchment paper on the pie dough and place your bean weights on top of the paper. Bake crust with bean weights for 8 minutes. Pull from the oven to remove weights by lifting up the parchment paper; bake for 4 more minutes. Remove from oven and turn down to 375°F.

FILLING

Over medium heat, add butter, leeks, and mushrooms to a skillet.
Cook until tender; set aside.

In a mixing bowl, whisk eggs together with garlic, ginger, flour, half-and-half, salt, and pepper. Add the leeks and mushrooms. Pour mixture into the par-baked pastry. Top with Parmesan. Bake the quiche at 375°F for 30–40 minutes until the eggs set. Let rest for 10 minutes before serving.

RECIPE CONTRIBUTED BY
Shanny Covey
Robin's Restaurant (p. 178)

KALE CHICKEN CAESAR SALAD

This is a sexy spin on the classic Caesar salad. This decadent salad has a rich, creamy dressing and the perfect amount of acid from the lemons, vinegar, and anchovies to cut right through it.

CAESAR DRESSING

3 egg yolks
1 cup Parmesan, finely grated
4 cloves of garlic
10 salt-packed anchovies, rinsed, filleted, and chopped finely
¼ cup cabernet vinegar
4 lemons, juiced
1 cup high-quality olive oil
(from Olea Farm, p. 159)
2 cups canola oil
salt and pepper

SALAD

1 bunch scarlet kale,
cleaned and torn into bite-size pieces
salt and pepper
4 oz. chicken, rotisserie or grilled
½ cup (+ 2 T per serving) hard sheep's milk cheese, grated
(from Rinconada Dairy, p. 177)
¼ cup Caesar dressing
½ red onion, thinly sliced into rings
¼ cup rough cut bread crumbs, toasted with olive oil
12 whole white anchovies

Yields 4 servings.

CAESAR DRESSING

Place yolks in a food processor with Parmesan, garlic, anchovies, vinegar, and lemon juice. Pulse to combine. Slowly emulsify in both oils. Season with salt and pepper.

SALAD

In a large bowl, season the kale with salt and pepper; add chicken and the grated cheese. Toss to combine. Dress the salad (approximately ¼ cup Caesar dressing) and divide among four plates. Garnish each plate with the remaining cheese, red onion, bread crumbs, and whole anchovies.

RECIPE CONTRIBUTED BY
Chris Kobayashi
Artisan (p. 150)

BLUE CHEESE, BACON, & ROASTED LEEK TARTINE

Oftentimes, I rip a hunk off this Little Red Hen blue cheese loaf while driving home from the market. I like to toast my tartine in bacon grease, top with roasted leeks, bacon bits, and—you guessed it—more blue cheese.

TARTINE

2 leeks, chopped
olive oil
salt and pepper
bacon
blue cheese bread, thickly sliced
(from Little Red Hen Bread, p. 162)
blue cheese

TARTINE

Preheat oven to 400°F. Chop leeks (white and pale green parts only) and place into a bowl with water. Wash thoroughly and drain water. Toss leeks with olive oil, salt, and pepper. Roast for 30–45 minutes until tender, every 15 minutes rotate the leeks with a spatula. Remove leeks from oven.

Fry bacon in a cast-iron skillet; set aside on a paper towel-lined plate. Once cool enough, chop into bite-size pieces. Toast the thickly sliced bread on both sides in the bacon drippings. Remove from heat. Pile on leeks, bacon bits, and crumbled blue cheese.

RECIPE CREATED BY
Kendra Aronson (p. 6)

WINTER CITRUS SALAD WITH AVOCADO, ALMONDS, & RADISH

This salad screams winter citrus: lemons, limes, oranges, and grapefruits! It's wonderfully hearty and great to enjoy in January after the face-stuffing, belly-busting holidays.

DRESSING

1 lemon
1 Meyer lemon
2 limes
2 oranges
1 grapefruit
1 large shallot, finely minced
2 T Champagne vinegar
⅓ cup grapeseed oil
⅓ cup extra virgin olive oil
salt and pepper

SALAD

8 beets
1 grapefruit, pithed and sliced
1 orange, pithed and sliced
4 ripe Hass avocados
salt and pepper
baby lettuce greens
¼ cup radishes, very finely sliced
½ cup almonds, sliced

Yields 8 servings.

DRESSING

To make the citrus vinaigrette, you will need a medium sized mixing bowl and a microplane grater. Zest all the citrus into a bowl. Add the shallots and vinegar. Squeeze the juice of the citrus over the shallots, taking care that no seeds fall into the bowl. Let the shallots and citrus macerate for 10 minutes. Slowly drizzle the oils into the bowl while continuously whisking. Once the oils have been added, season the dressing with salt and pepper. Taste. Adjust the seasoning—if it is not tart enough, add a dash more vinegar. It is best to refrigerate for 30 minutes before using.

SALAD

Preheat oven to 450°F. Remove the tops from the beets and wash them under cold running water. Place them in a shallow baking dish along with 1 cup of water. Tightly cover the baking dish with aluminum foil and bake them in the oven for 40 minutes. Carefully remove the dish from the oven to check if they are ready. Use a paring knife to test the beets by poking them. If the knife slides in and out with ease, the beets are done. Peel the skins from the beets, cut into bite-size wedges. Place the beets into a mixing bowl and dress them lightly with some of the citrus vinaigrette. Allow them to marinate for 30 minutes.

» To assemble the salad you will need a large platter. Lay down the segments of grapefruit and oranges. Remove the pits and skins from the avocados, cut them into ½-inch slices. Arrange the slices however you like and then season with salt and pepper. Scatter the beets over the top of the avocado and drizzle the vinaigrette over the beets. Lightly dress the greens and radish with the vinaigrette and delicately mound them on top of the avocado, citrus segments, and beets. Sprinkle the almonds over the salad; serve immediately.

"Other optional toppings such as goat cheese, toasted nuts, or sliced fennel are delicious, too," says Brian, Chef/Owner of Ember Restaurant (p. 157).

RECIPE CONTRIBUTED BY

Brian Collins
Ember Restaurant (p. 157)

SALAD WITH APPLES, CELERY, & HERBED BLUE CHEESE DRESSING

This is a fun Central California twist on the classic Waldorf salad: sweet butter lettuce, SLOcally grown apples, crunchy celery, toasted walnuts, and herbed blue cheese dressing.

DRESSING

1 cup buttermilk
2 cups aïoli or mayonnaise
1 T lemon juice
½ t. Worcestershire sauce
2 t. garlic, minced
½ t. salt
½ T pink peppercorns, crushed
1 cup blue cheese, crumbled
2 T scallions or chives
½ cup parsley, chopped

Yields approximately 1 quart.

SALAD

1 apple (choose your favorite variety), cored and roughly chopped
¼ cup celery, chopped
¼ cup celery leaf, chopped
¼ cup walnuts, toasted and chopped
1 oz. herbed blue cheese dressing
3–4 butter lettuce leaves
pepper

Yields 1 serving.

DRESSING

In a large stainless steel bowl, combine and whisk all ingredients until fully incorporated. Store and refrigerate after use.

SALAD

In a large bowl, combine the apple, celery, celery leaf, walnuts, and dressing. Using a spoon, toss the ingredients together. Place the mixture on a bed of butter leaf and top with a little freshly cracked black pepper.

RECIPE CONTRIBUTED BY
Shaun Behrens
Luna Red Restaurant•Bar (p. 164)

VEGAN CREAM OF HARD SQUASH & MUSHROOM SOUP WITH QUINOA

"Creating a vegan mushroom soup that appealed en masse *at the market was one of the hardest nuts to crack. The sweet creaminess of the hard winter squash with the richness of good mushrooms and light protein (quinoa) made this soup the winner!"*

SOUP

1 lb. mushrooms
1 t. salt
(any hearty, meaty variety)
olive oil
3 cloves of garlic, chopped
2 sprigs of thyme
3 stalks of celery, diced
2 carrots, diced
1 small onion, diced
3 oz. white wine
2 lbs. of hard winter squash
(Kabocha, Butternut, or Blue Hubbard;
peeled, seeded, and chopped
into 1-inch pieces)
6 cups vegetable stock
1 cup quinoa
1 bayleaf
salt and pepper

SOUP

Clean and slice your mushrooms. In a large stock pot, salt the mushrooms and sauté in olive oil along with the garlic and thyme until they are golden brown. Remove from the pot. Add a little bit more olive oil and put in your *mirepoix*—celery, carrots, and onions. Add salt and sauté over medium heat until the onions are translucent.

Add the white wine to deglaze the pot. Add the winter squash, stock, and half of the mushrooms. Bring to a boil until the squash is soft enough to blend. With an immersion blender, blend in the pot until smooth. The consistency should be a semi-thick broth.

Add the quinoa, bayleaf, and the remaining mushrooms; bring back to a boil. Reduce to a simmer and cook until the quinoa pops, the fiber will uncurl and the soup will become thicker. Remove the bayleaf; salt and pepper to taste. Soup keeps for 7–10 days in the refrigerator.

RECIPE CONTRIBUTED BY
Alyx Gille
Good Tides Organic Bistro (p. 160)

MINESTRONE ALLA GENOVESE

For this classic Italian soup, I suggest having everything mise en place*—a French culinary phrase which means "putting in place." In other words, have all your ingredients prepped and arranged accordingly.*

MINESTRONE

½ lb. dried white beans, rinsed
½ t. salt
¼ lb. pancetta, chopped
⅓ cup olive oil
1 onion, chopped
1 large carrot, cut into ½-inch dice
1 rib of celery, cut into ½-inch dice
3 cloves of garlic, finely minced
2 zucchini, cut into ½-inch dice
¼ lb. green beans, trimmed at both ends and cut into ½-inch pieces
½ lb. boiled potatoes, peeled and cut into ¾-inch dice
4 cups shredded Savoy cabbage
½ lb. kale, rinsed, drained, stems discarded, leaves chopped (≈ 6 cups)
28 oz. can tomatoes, chopped and drained well
4½ cups chicken broth
salt and pepper
1 T of pesto

MINESTRONE

In a large bowl, let the white beans soak overnight in enough water to cover them by 2 inches. Drain the white beans. In a saucepan combine them with enough water to cover them by 2 inches, and simmer uncovered, adding more water if necessary to keep them barely covered, for 45 minutes to 1 hour, or until they are tender. Add the salt and simmer the white beans for 5 minutes more. Remove the saucepan from the heat and let the beans stand uncovered.

In a large pot, cook the pancetta (Italian cured pork belly) in the olive oil over moderate heat, stirring until it is crispy and pale golden. Then add the onion; cook the mixture, stirring, until onion is soft. Add the carrots, the celery, and the garlic; cook the mixture, stirring for 4 minutes. Add the zucchini, the green beans, and the potatoes; cook the mixture, stirring for another 4 minutes. Add the cabbage and the kale; stirring until the cabbage is wilted. Add the tomatoes and the broth; simmer the soup covered for 1 hour.

Drain the white beans, reserving the liquid. In a blender or food processor, purée half of the beans with 1 cup of the reserved liquid; stir the purée and the remaining white beans into the soup. Simmer the soup uncovered for 15 minutes. Thin the soup (if desired) with some of the remaining reserved liquid; season with salt and pepper. Add the pesto before serving.

RECIPE CONTRIBUTED BY
Nicola Allegretta
Mama's Meatball (p. 165)

MIND-BLOWING MILK-BRAISED PORK

Good things take time... prepare to have your mind blown by this succulent, milk-braised pork! Roasted quince is a great side for this dish, as are figs, fennel, potatoes, or sunchokes.

PORK

3-5 lbs. pork shoulder
sea salt and pepper
fresh thyme, chopped
1-2 heads of garlic
1 head of fennel
1 lemon
sprigs of thyme
2-3 fresh bay leaves
1 gallon of milk

PORK

Buy the highest quality pork shoulder available, de-boned, bone-in, or tied into a roast—it doesn't matter. It should weigh about three to five pounds. Rub the pork generously with sea salt, freshly cracked pepper, and chopped thyme. Let it sit uncovered in your refrigerator overnight.

The next day, remove it from the refrigerator and let it rest on the counter for at least an hour while you preheat your oven to 325°F.

Place the room temperature pork in a deep cast-iron skillet. Add two heads of garlic sliced in half crosswise to expose the core, a head of roughly chopped fennel, a few slices of lemon, a few sprigs of thyme, and a couple bay leaves. Pour milk into the deep cast-iron skillet until approximately half of the shoulder is submerged. Note: there may not be enough room for all the milk so just add what you can. You will be able to add more later during the cooking process.

Place it in the pre-heated oven and let it braise uncovered for about four hours. Every 30–45 minutes turn the shoulder over into the milk so that the surface that was exposed to the heat is now submerged in the milk. Baste generously and add more milk as needed.

"It doesn't start out as much, but by the fourth or fifth flip something glorious happens. The milk will eventually break down and the meat will start to caramelize. Because the milk separates into fat and solids, the shoulder basically slow cooks itself in flavored fat. The best way to make sure it is ready is to pierce the roast at the thickest point with a sharp knife and the knife should slide in and out without any resistance. If the knife gently glides in and then easily out, your work is done," says Chef Jensen (p. 154).

RECIPE CONTRIBUTED BY
Chef Jensen Lorenzen
Formerly of The Cass House
Inn & Restaurant (p. 154)

CIOPPINO

I had always been too intimidated to make my own Cioppino—but really, it's as easy as cooking loads of seafood in a huge stock pot with a bunch of spices and tomato sauces. Impress your friends with this stew!

CIOPPINO

½ cup olive oil
2 medium onions, diced
2 stalks of celery, diced
2 T parsley, chopped
2 cloves of garlic, diced
28 oz. canned diced tomatoes
8 oz. tomato sauce
half bottle of your favorite hot sauce
1 cup water
1 bay leaf
1 t. dried basil
1 t. dried rosemary
1 t. dried oregano
½ cup port wine
½ cup white wine
2 crabs, cracked
16 raw shrimp
16 clams in the shell
¾ lb. white fish

Note: any combination of fish and shellfish will work!

CIOPPINO

In a large stock pot, heat the olive oil over medium heat. Sauté the onions, celery, parsley, and garlic for 5 minutes until the vegetables are translucent. Add the diced tomatoes, tomato sauce, hot sauce, water, and spices. Add wine, then stir everything. Cook for 20 minutes, stirring occasionally.

Next, add the crab, shrimp, and clams, and top off the mixture with water so that all the seafood is submerged. Cover and simmer for 20 minutes.

Add the white fish on top of the stew, continue to simmer for another 10 minutes, stirring occasionally.

Serve hot in a bowl with a slab of crusty bread. Wear a bib—it's messy!

Note from Margie: "Cioppino is traditionally served in Italy for Christmas."

RECIPE CONTRIBUTED BY
Margie Hurd
Formerly of SLO Fresh Catch

OLIVE OIL CAKE WITH MEYER LEMON CURD & CRÈME FRAÎCHE

Ten years ago Chef Julie came to California for a few months to visit her aunt and uncle's olive oil farm in Templeton—and she never left! Enjoy her sweet homage to Olea olive oil with this cake.

WHIPPED CRÈME FRAÎCHE

2 cups heavy cream
2 T buttermilk
½ cup of granulated sugar

OLIVE OIL CAKE

2 cups all-purpose flour
1 ¾ cups sugar plus 2 T for dusting
1 ½ t. salt
½ t. baking soda
½ t. baking powder
1 ⅓ cups Olea Farm's Arbequina olive oil
1 ¼ cups whole milk
3 eggs
juice and zest of two oranges

MEYER LEMON CURD

4 large egg yolks
½ cup of granulated sugar
zest of 4 Meyer lemons
⅓ cup of Meyer lemon juice
⅛ t. salt
6 T butter, melted

WHIPPED CRÈME FRAÎCHE

In a container with a lid, stir together the heavy cream and buttermilk. Cover and let sit at room temperature for 24 hours. The cream will take on a wonderful aroma—gently soured and thickened. Then refrigerate for the crème fraîche to set.

OLIVE OIL CAKE

Preheat oven to 350°F. Prepare a 9-inch cake pan by oiling it lightly and dusting with two tablespoons of sugar. Set aside. Stir the dry ingredients in a large bowl. Whisk together the wet ingredients in a separate bowl. Make a well in the dry ingredients and pour in the wet ingredients. Stir until just combined. Pour into the cake pan and bake for about 40 minutes. To test the cake, insert a toothpick and pull it out. If it comes out clean, remove cake from the oven.

MEYER LEMON CURD

You will need to prepare the curd over a *bain marie*. In order to do so, fill a medium-size saucepan with a couple inches of water over medium heat. Whisk all the egg yolks, sugar, zest, lemon juice, and salt into a large mixing bowl and place it over the steaming bath. The water should be simmering, not boiling; do not let the bowl touch the water. Whisk constantly until the yolks thicken, approximately 7–10 minutes. Pull whisk up out of curd, and if it creates a ribbon, then the curd is ready. Remove from the heat, stir in the butter, and set aside to cool.

» When ready to assemble, pour the crème fraîche in a standup mixer and whisk to soft peaks with sugar. Serve in mason jar, in this order: olive oil cake, lemon curd, whipped crème fraîche.

RECIPE CONTRIBUTED BY

Julie Simon
Foremost Wine Co. (p. 159)

APPLE CRISP WITH BROWN SUGAR & OAT CRUMBLE

For a fun family outing, visit SLO Creek Farms during their "u-pick" season. Fill up your bushels with Braeburn apples, bake this crisp, and enjoy the fruits of your labor!

APPLE CRISP

10 cups apples, peeled, cored, and sliced
(from SLO Creek Farms, p. 183)
1 cup granulated sugar
1 T all-purpose flour
1 t. ground cinnamon
½ cup water
1 cup quick-cooking oats
1 cup all-purpose flour
1 cup packed brown sugar
¼ t. baking powder
¼ t. baking soda
½ cup butter, melted

APPLE CRISP

Preheat oven to 350°F. Place the sliced apples in a 8x8 inch pan. Mix the sugar, flour, and ground cinnamon together; sprinkle over apples. Pour water evenly over apples.

Combine the oats, flour, brown sugar, baking powder, baking soda, and melted butter together in a bowl; mix with your hands until it reaches a crumbly consistency. Crumble evenly over the apple mixture. Bake at 350°F for about 45 minutes. Let stand for 10 minutes before serving.

Kendra's suggestion: serve à la mode with the vanilla sheep's milk ice cream from Negranti Creamery (p. 169).

RECIPE CONTRIBUTED BY
Gable Family
SLO Creek Farms (p. 183)

BUTTERSCOTCH PUDDING WITH PECAN BISCOTTI & CARAMEL SAUCE

"Synergy is the creation of a whole that is greater than the simple sum of its parts." I think of this Aristotle quotation when creating (and enjoying) this decadent trio of pudding, biscotti, and caramel.

BUTTERSCOTCH PUDDING

7 oz. egg yolks
½ cup brown sugar
6 T unsalted butter
half of a vanilla bean
3½ cups heavy cream
1 cup brown sugar
¼ cup water
1 t. salt

Yields 12 servings.

PECAN BISCOTTI

½ cup unsalted butter
¾ cup brown sugar
3 large eggs
1 t. vanilla
1 t. baking powder
¾ t. salt
3 cups all-purpose flour
1 cup chopped pecans, toasted
1 cup Valrhona Dulcey blond chocolate chips, rough cut

Yields ≈ 60 mini biscotti.

CRÈME FRAÎCHE CARAMEL SAUCE

½ cup water
2 cups sugar
¼ cup corn syrup
1 cup heavy cream, warm
½ cup crème fraîche
2 T sugar
1 t. lemon juice
1 t. salt

Yields 2½ cups.

BUTTERSCOTCH PUDDING

Preheat oven to 275°F. In a bowl, combine yolks and ½ cup brown sugar. Whisk to combine and set aside.

Heat a medium-size saucepan over medium-high heat. Caramelize the butter with the vanilla bean until deep golden, be careful not to burn.

Pour the heavy cream into it's own mixing bowl to prep it for tempering. (Tempering is slowly bringing up the temperature of an ingredient sensitive to heat to prevent it from curdling, breaking, or cooking too fast.) Therefore, add a small portion of the caramelized vanilla butter into the heavy cream while stirring continuously. Then, add this entire mixture back into the saucepan.

In a separate medium-size pot, place 1 cup brown sugar and add a ¼ cup of water; swirl to dissolve the sugar. Bring to a boil over medium-high heat and caramelize until deep brown. The sugar will start to smoke and burn—don't be alarmed when your smoke alarm goes off! This is what gives this pudding the desired flavor. Once the sugar is highly caramelized, whisk in the cream and butter mixture until combined. Stir in salt.

Temper in the bowl of yolks and brown sugar by adding a small portion of the warmed mixture, stirring continuously, then add to the saucepan.

Divide into twelve 6 oz. ramekins and bake in a 275°F oven with a water bath for 45–55 minutes or until lightly browned.

PECAN BISCOTTI

Preheat oven to 325°F. Line a sheet pan with parchment paper. In a mixing bowl, mix together the butter and sugar; then add the eggs one at a time, beating well after each addition and scraping down the bowl midway through. Mix in the vanilla, baking powder, and salt. Mix in the flour, 1 cup at a time, until you have a cohesive, well-blended dough. Add the nuts and Dulcey chips, mixing until they are well-distributed throughout the dough.

Transfer the dough to a work surface. Divide it into two fairly equal pieces and shape each piece into a rough 18 inches log. Transfer the logs to the prepared baking sheets, leaving about 3 inches between each log; you may or may not need to use both baking sheets. Wet your fingers with water and pat the logs into smooth-topped rectangles 18 inches long x 2½ inches wide and 1-inch thick.

Bake the logs for 20–25 minutes, or until they're beginning to brown around the edges. Remove them from the oven; allow to cool for 30 minutes. Lower the oven temperature to 275°F. Gently transfer the logs to a cutting surface and use a serrated knife to cut them on the diagonal into ¼-inch wide slices. "Because of the nuts and the nature of the dough, the biscotti at this point are prone to crumbling; just be sure to use a slow, gentle sawing motion, and accept the fact that some bits and pieces will break off. It's the privilege of the cook to eat these warm, tasty bits and pieces as they're created," says Chef Chris (p. 150).

Carefully transfer the slices to a parchment-lined baking sheet. You can crowd them together as they won't expand further—about a ¼-inch breathing space is all that's required.

Return the biscotti to the 275°F oven and bake them for 20–30 minutes until they're very dry and beginning to brown—not too dark. Remove them from the oven, cool completely, and store in an airtight container.

CRÈME FRAÎCHE CARAMEL SAUCE

In a saucepan, heat water, sugar, and corn syrup until medium dark while stirring occasionally. Then whisk in cream, crème fraîche, sugar, and lemon juice. Although the mixture may bubble and splatter, keep whisking until the sauce thickens. Remove from heat and stir in salt. Allow to cool before serving. Store in a glass jar.

» Pour a layer of caramel crème fraîche sauce over the butterscotch pudding. Serve with biscotti and whipped cream (if desired).

RECIPE CONTRIBUTED BY

Chris Kobayashi
Artisan (p. 150)

SUPPORT
YOUR
SLOCAL
FARMER!

SPRING

VEGGIE OMELETTE

Start your day off right with this vegetable-packed omelette—farm fresh eggs, tomatoes, zucchini, squash, asparagus, onion, bell peppers, mushrooms, spinach, avocado, and cheddar cheese.

OMELETTE

12 eggs
2 T grapeseed oil
2 T butter (½ T per omelette)
½ cup Roma tomatoes, diced
½ cup zucchini, diced
½ cup Crookneck squash, diced
½ cup asparagus, cut into 1-inch pieces
½ cup yellow onion, diced
¼ cup red bell pepper, diced
¼ cup green bell pepper, diced
1 cup Cremini mushrooms, sliced
1 cup Bloomsdale spinach, chopped
1 cup mild cheddar cheese, shredded
1 avocado, quartered and fanned
salt and pepper

Yields 4 omelettes.

OMELETTE

Whip eggs in a bowl with a balloon whisk until slightly aerated and set aside. Heat a large, non-stick sauté pan over medium-high heat. Add grapeseed oil; once it is hot, add all of the vegetables one at a time and sauté until the water is sweated out and they are lightly caramelized. Season with salt and pepper to taste, and set aside on a paper towel to drain excess liquid.

Heat four medium-sized non-stick sauté pans over medium heat, then add a half tablespoon of butter to each pan. Evenly distribute the whipped eggs into the four pans. With a high-heat silicone spatula, push the solidifying eggs onto one side of the pan, hold at an angle, and let the liquid eggs drain to bottom. This helps to cook eggs quickly and evenly. Reduce heat to low.

Equally divide the cooked vegetables onto the top of the eggs, add the cheese, and fold the omelet in half over itself. Slide the omelettes onto four plates and garnish with the fanned avocado halves.

RECIPE CONTRIBUTED BY
Chris Manning
Thomas Hill Organics (p. 188)

BEEKEEPER BURRATA

"This dish is very dear to my heart as the burrata is dressed with some of the best produce grown or harvested within 30 miles of Foremost Wine Co.—it is conceptualized around terroir *and its beauty reigns it its simplicity."*

BURRATA

4 oz. burrata
4–8 small pieces of honeycomb
2 T Arbequina olive oil
smoked sea salt
1 t. finely minced rosemary
2 T marcona almonds, roasted
½ cup fresh mulberries
a few edible flowers such as viola, nasturtium, salvia, borage, calendula, or cornflower

BURRATA

Cut the burrata in thirds and place it on a plate. Interval with small pieces of honeycomb, drizzle with olive oil, and sprinkle every item with the smoked sea salt and rosemary. Garnish with almonds, mulberries, and edible flowers.

Chef Julie's tip: "Serve with some grilled levain bread and a bottle of local Claiborne & Churchill Estate Dry Riesling."

RECIPE CONTRIBUTED BY
Julie Simon
Foremost Wine Co. (p. 159)

HUEVOS RANCHEROS

Prepare your breakfast eggs how you like 'em—fried, sunny side up, scrambled, poached. Place your eggs on top of breakfast potatoes, beans, or fresh tortilla chips, then smother generously with this ranchero sauce!

RANCHERO SAUCE

½ cup grapeseed oil
6 cloves of garlic, chopped
6 jalapeños, sliced
1 can chipotles in adobo sauce
2 lbs. heirloom tomatoes
1 bunch of cilantro, chopped
salt and pepper

RANCHERO SAUCE

In a stock pot on medium heat, add oil, garlic, and jalapeños. Once caramelized, add the can of chipotles, tomatoes, cilantro, salt, and pepper.

Let it simmer for 2 hours until the tomatoes have stewed down and have busted open. Keep stirring a few times every hour.

Should yield two 24 oz. mason jars. Will keep in the fridge for 48 hours.

RECIPE CONTRIBUTED BY
Chef Liz Lynch

1
2
3
4
5
6

SPROUTS GUIDE

This is a go-to guide for sprouts and some inspirational tips on how to incorporate them into your favorite dishes!

SPROUTS
salad sprout mix
pea sprouts
radish sprouts
fenugreek sprouts
clover sprouts
sunflower sprouts

SPROUTS

"Nature works in amazing ways. All the nutrients needed for a new plant to grow are contained in the seed. These nutrients remain inactive until sprouted. Once sprouted, the sprout becomes a nutrient powerhouse with highly concentrated sources of vitamins, minerals, enzymes, amino acids, and other nutrients that are hard to find elsewhere. Many times eating the sprout is more nutritious than the full-grown vegetable," says Julia of Mt. Olive Organic Farm (p. 168). Below she explains how she enjoys her sprouts.

1. SALAD SPROUT MIX
This is a mix of a few different beans and lentils: adzuki, lentil, pea, and mung. This mix is a great addition to any salad if you are want to add a little extra protein crunch while boosting your Vitamin A, B, C, and E levels.

2. PEA SPROUTS
These taste just like snow peas. They are quite versatile; add them to your omelettes, sandwiches, salads, and stir frys.

3. RADISH SPROUTS
Definitely the spiciest sprout of the bunch—it's got a little peppery bite to it! These are really good in sandwiches or egg dishes.

4. FENUGREEK SPROUTS
Although these sprouts don't have a strong flavor, they have many health benefits. Many new mothers snack on fenugreek sprouts (or take fenugreek supplements) as they naturally increase breast milk production. Fenugreek sprouts are great for those with asthma or allergies since they aid in digestion and help respiratory systems.

5. CLOVER SPROUTS
These are the most mild of the bunch and very similar to alfalfa sprouts. They have similar flavor profiles but last a little bit longer in the fridge. Sprinkle on salads.

6. SUNFLOWER SPROUTS
A personal favorite! They are nutty and have a hearty crunch to them. I love snacking on them raw or adding them to bagels with cream cheese.

SPROUT INSPIRATION CONTRIBUTED BY
Julia Ng
Mt. Olive Organic Farm (p. 168)

WARM BUTTERED OYSTERS OVER YOUNG GREENS

This decadent side salad reminds me of springtime in Paris: warm, wonderful, buttery oysters, toasted crostini, and delicate young greens. Enhance this dish by using an interesting salad mix such as purslane and arugula.

OYSTERS
5 T butter
1 minced shallot
3 T sherry vinegar
2 dozen fresh oysters, scrubbed and shucked
mixed young salad greens
salt and pepper

CROSTINI
half loaf French bread

Yields 4 servings.

OYSTERS

Melt half of the butter in a skillet and sauté the shallot until it begins to brown. Add the vinegar and reduce by half. Add the remaining butter and oysters, stirring and tossing until the oysters are plump and firmed and the butter is incorporated into the *beurre blanc*.

CROSTINI

Make crostini in any manner you like—brush with olive oil and toast, broil, barbecue, or bake.

» Serve by creating a salad on each plate. Top the greens with the warm oysters (6 per plate) and the butter "dressing". Season with salt and pepper. Serve immediately with crostini on the side.

RECIPE CONTRIBUTED BY
Greg Holt
Big Sky Cafe (p. 152)

SHRIMP SPRING ROLLS WITH CHILI SAUCE & GINGER SOY SAUCE

Invite your friends over for a spring roll making party: set up a nice assembly line with duties like shrimp sautéer, vegetable prepper, sauce maker... with an all-star team you'll be whipping these rolls out in no time.

SHRIMP

50 raw shrimp (≈ 10 lbs.)
3 T canola oil
14 oz. Sriracha sauce
½ t. salt
1 t. pepper

NOODLES

8 oz. cellophane noodles
sesame oil

VIETNAMESE CHILI SAUCE

½ T garlic, minced
½ T ginger, minced
½ cup lime juice, freshly squeezed
⅓ cup sugar
⅛ cup Nuac Mam (fish sauce)
½ T red chili flakes
⅛ cup Sriracha sauce
2 T sesame oil
1½ cups canola oil

GINGER SOY DIPPING SAUCE

16 oz. dark brown sugar
2 cups soy sauce
½ cup ginger, minced
3 t. unseasoned rice vinegar

PER ROLL

1 rice paper
1 red lettuce leaf
bunch of cellophane noodles
5 shrimp
1 avocado slice
1 cucumber slice, peeled, seeded, sliced
5 carrot sticks, peeled, julienned
5 daikon sticks, peeled, julienned
1 t. mint, chopped
1 t. cilantro, chopped

SHRIMP

Sauté the shrimp in canola oil. When halfway cooked, drain any excess liquid. Add Sriracha, salt, and pepper; finish cooking. Turn onto sheet pan and transfer to refrigerator.

NOODLES

Place cellophane noodles in boiling water and cook like pasta. Stir frequently for 3–4 minutes until soft but not mushy. Drain and rinse with cold water. Once cooled, coat with sesame oil so they won't stick together.

VIETNAMESE CHILI SAUCE

Blend all ingredients except the canola oil in a blender. Then, slowly blend in the canola oil until emulsified.

GINGER SOY DIPPING SAUCE

In a medium saucepan, combine the sugar and soy sauce. Heat slowly until the sugar dissolves. Once dissolved, simmer for 5 minutes. Remove from heat, add the ginger, and let steep for 5 minutes. Strain the liquid through a fine cheesecloth, then add and stir in the vinegar. Chill the sauce before use.

PER ROLL

Dip rice paper briefly in hot water; pat dry. Place one leaf of lettuce in the center. Spread a small bunch of cooked noodles on the lettuce leaf; place shrimp evenly. Continue with the rest of the ingredients, making sure everything is evenly dispersed and only resting on the lettuce. Roll gently like a burrito. If not serving immediately, wrap in plastic wrap and refrigerate. Will keep up to 2 hours in the fridge. Serve with Vietnamese chili sauce and ginger soy dipping sauce. Yields 10 rolls.

RECIPE CONTRIBUTED BY

Robin Covey
Novo Restaurant & Lounge (p. 171)

BURRATA SALAD WITH SWEET PEAS, SNAP PEAS, & SUGAR PEAS

When peas come into season, I squeal with joy that I get to create this dish. This salad calls for three types of fresh peas, vibrant greens, a citrusy vinaigrette, and a creamy ball of burrata.

LEMON VINAIGRETTE

3 T fresh lemon juice
1 T shallot
1 t. Dijon mustard
zest of 1 lemon
dash of honey
sprig of thyme
½ cup olive oil
salt and pepper

SALAD

arugula
English sweet peas
sugar peas
snap peas
asparagus, shaved
burrata
mint
salt and pepper

LEMON VINAIGRETTE

In a food processor, blend together all the ingredients, except the oil. Then slowly pour in the oil while blending until smooth. Season with salt and pepper.

SALAD

In a mixing bowl, toss together arugula, peas, asparagus—choose the proportions and quantities to your liking. Lightly dress the salad with the vinaigrette. Plate the salad, cut the burrata in half, and place in the middle. Drizzle vinaigrette over burrata. Garnish with fresh mint, salt, and pepper.

RECIPE CONTRIBUTED BY
Jen Manuele
Sally Loo's (p. 181)

MISO GLAZED BLACK COD WITH ZUCCHINI "NOODLES" & BLOSSOMS

"This is a classic Japanese recipe that has become such a Californian staple to me. Black cod is a very sustainable catch from our very own coast. Source the Asian ingredients at the San Luis Oriental Market on Monterey Street."

COD

¼ cup of mirin
¼ cup sake
3 T brown sugar
4 T white miso
¼ cup grapeseed oil
2 lbs. of black cod, skin on or off
1 T grapeseed oil
2 garlic cloves, smashed
1 t. of chili flakes
2 t. ginger, grated
2 T chives, thinly minced
chive blossoms, for garnish

DASHI

4 cups of water
1 piece of kombu
1 cup of bonito flakes
2 t. salt
¼ cup of mirin

ZUCCHINI "NOODLES" & BLOSSOMS

8 zucchini
1 basket zucchini blossoms
salt

Yields 4 servings.

RECIPE CONTRIBUTED BY

Julie Simon
Foremost Wine Co. (p.159)

COD

Bring the mirin (sweet rice wine vinegar) and sake to a boil for the alcohol to evaporate, then whisk in sugar and miso. Remove from the heat and add the grapeseed oil. When cold, place the fish and the miso glaze in a Ziploc bag and refrigerate for up to 3 days. "The marinade will act as a quick cure which allows the fish to firm a bit without compromising its silky and buttery awesomeness," says Chef Julie of Foremost Wine Co. (p. 159).

DASHI

What is dashi you ask? "Dashi is a sea-like broth." Bring the water and kombu (dried kelp) to a gentle simmer, add the bonito flakes (dried and shaved bonito fish). Turn off heat and let steep for 30 minutes. Strain through a fine mesh; season to taste with salt and mirin.

ZUCCHINI "NOODLES" & BLOSSOMS

Tip from Julie: "A Japanese mandolin would be essential to achieve the remarkably delicate zucchini 'noodle'; it's a great kitchen investment." Choose young and firm zucchini, slice lengthwise on the mandolin to yield about a quart and a half in volume. Cut the zucchini blossoms in half; remove pistils.

» "If all your ingredients are *mise en place*, everything will be quick and easy—making this dish ideal for dinner parties. Have your oven on broil and a fish spatula at the ready. Dashi should be warmed and ready to ladle. Have everything ready to sautée with a pair of tongs and four shallow plates." Ready? Go! Place the cod on a baking sheet and slide in the oven. If the broiler is really strong, the middle shelf of the oven will be adequate. Place a large sautée pan on medium-high heat. Coat the bottom with grapeseed oil, add the garlic, and let toast lightly to extract the aroma, then discard. Add the chili flakes and ginger; stir. Add the zucchini "noodles", sauté, salt to taste; add the zucchini blossoms, sauté, and remove from heat. Add the chives. Ladle two ounces of dashi in each shallow plate; divide the zucchini "noodles" and zucchini blossoms into the middle of each plate. Pull the black cod from the oven—it should have a nice blackened crust and just about to flake. Using a spatula, place gently over the zucchini "noodles" and zucchini blossoms; garnish with chive blossoms.

SEA BASS OVER MARKET GREENS AND VEGGIES WITH BASIL DRESSING

This mouth-watering sea bass tastes as good as it looks. The sweet pea tendrils and asparagus give a nod to springtime, while the beets, avocado, and garlicky basil dressing hint that summer is just around the corner!

SALAD
5 leaves of butter leaf lettuce
2 small handfuls of Bloomsdale spinach
8 sweet pea tendrils
4 golden beets
8 small spears of asparagus

SEA BASS
(2) 6 oz. portions of sea bass*
salt and pepper
olive oil

DRESSING
¼ cup olive oil
⅛ cup canola oil or sunflower oil
3 cloves of garlic, minced
⅛ cup lemon juice, fresh squeezed
1 t. salt
1 t. black pepper
1½ cups basil leaves, stems removed and washed
1 t. sugar (optional)

VEGETABLES
10 cherry tomatoes, sliced
1 half avocado, sliced
2 small yellow carrots, peeled

*This recipe works well with most fish if sea bass is unavailable.

Yields 2 servings.

RECIPE CONTRIBUTED BY
Ben Richardson
Novo Restaurant & Lounge (p.170)

SALAD

Wash and dry your butter lettuce, spinach, and sweet pea tendrils. Remove the larger stems from the spinach and sweet pea tendrils. Tear all of your greens into a mixing bowl; cover and refrigerate.

In a small stock pot, simmer the beets until fork tender. When they are fully cooked, remove from the heat. Rinse under cool water and remove the skin. Refrigerate the beets uncovered until cool. Slice the beets into small wedges and set aside.

The asparagus can be roasted, blanched, or grilled depending on your preference. Once cool enough to handle, slice into small pieces, set aside.

SEA BASS

Preheat oven to 375°F. Season your fish with salt and pepper. In a sauté pan, heat a small amount of olive oil and sear the fish. Turn the fish over and bake in the oven until the fish is cooked through—cooking time may vary depending on the size or type of fish, usually between 10–12 minutes.

DRESSING

Place the oils, garlic, lemon juice, salt, and pepper into a blender. Blend until smooth and emulsified. Add the basil leaves one at a time initially so they have a chance to incorporate into the dressing. Once the dressing begins to thin out a bit, you can add the remaining basil. Continue to blend the dressing until smooth. You may add the sugar to your dressing at this point if desired. It is also optional to add a touch more lemon juice to bring up the overall acidity. Adjust seasoning with salt and pepper to taste.

VEGETABLES

Toss your greens and asparagus with a small amount of the basil dressing and separate the mix onto two plates. Arrange your beets, sliced tomatoes, and sliced avocado in and around your salad. Tip from Chef Ben: "I prefer to add these ingredients after the salad is dressed so the colors stay nice and bright." Cut carrots into a fine *julienne*. Place carrots on the top of the salad followed by your sea bass. Finish the salad with more dressing over the fish.

POLLO SALTIMBOCCA

"I enjoy cooking with wine, sometimes I even put it in the food!"—Julia Child. Take a hint from Julia: pour yourself a nice glass of chilled white wine and reserve just enough for this delightful recipe.

CHICKEN

(4) 6 oz. skinless, boneless chicken breast
salt and pepper
8 large sage leaves
4 thin slices Prosciutto di Parma
all-purpose flour, for dusting
2 T olive oil
4 T unsalted butter, cut into tablespoons
¼ cup plus 2 T dry white wine
1 cup chicken stock
sage leaves for garnish (optional)

Yields 4 servings.

CHICKEN

Halve, butterfly, and lightly pound the chicken breast. Season the chicken with salt and pepper. Place 2 sage leaves on each breast. Top with a slice of prosciutto, trimming it to fit. Press the prosciutto to help it adhere to the chicken. Dust the chicken with flour, shaking off the excess.

Heat a large skillet. Add the oil and 2 tablespoons of the butter. Add 2 of the breasts, prosciutto side up, and cook over high heat until nearly cooked through, about 3 minutes. Turn the chicken and cook just until the prosciutto begins to shrink, about 1 minute. Transfer the chicken to a plate; repeat with the remaining chicken. Pour off any fat and wipe out the skillet.

Add the remaining butter to the skillet. Add the wine and cook over high heat until reduced by half, about 2 minutes. Add the stock and bring to a boil. Cook until reduced by half, about 3 minutes.

Return the chicken to the skillet, prosciutto side up, and simmer over moderate heat until the chicken is cooked through, about 2 minutes; season with salt and pepper. Transfer the chicken to individual plates, pour the sauce on top, and serve. Optional: add more sage leaves for garnish.

RECIPE CONTRIBUTED BY
Nicola Allegretta
Mama's Meatball (p. 165)

QUAIL SALAD WITH SHERRY VINAIGRETTE

This beautifully seared quail rests on a bed of bitter greens, dressed in a rich bacon sherry vinaigrette. You will truly feel like a skilled chef making this dish!

SHERRY VINAIGRETTE

3 shallots, finely diced
12 oz. sherry vinegar
5 T brown sugar
1 T Dijon mustard
1 t. salt
1 pint bacon fat, melted

QUAIL

3 T olive oil
4 quail, semi-boneless
salt and pepper
2 T butter

SALAD

2 heads of Belgian endive, leaves only
1 head of Treviso, leaves torn
1 head of blonde frisée, stem removed
¼ cup lardons, cooked
2 T pine nuts, toasted
¼ cup Feta cheese, crumbled

Yields 4 servings.

SHERRY VINAIGRETTE

Sweat shallots on medium heat in a sauce pot until caramelized. Add the sherry vinegar and reduce by half. Pour the liquid into a food processor, let cool for 15 minutes. Add the sugar, mustard, and salt. Turn on the food processor and slowly add bacon fat until emulsified.

QUAIL

Heat olive oil in a large sauté pan over high heat. Season the quail with salt and pepper. Sear the quail breast-side down until caramelized, reduce heat to medium; add the butter, flip, and cook for roughly 2 minutes, basting the quail the entire time with a spoon. Set aside in a warm place on a paper towel.

SALAD

Toss the endive, Treviso, frisée, bacon lardons, pine nuts, and feta cheese in a medium sized bowl. Toss with desired amount of warm sherry vinaigrette.

» Evenly divide the salad onto four plates. Place a quail on top of each salad and serve immediately.

RECIPE CONTRIBUTED BY
Chris Manning
Thomas Hill Organics (p. 188)

AVOCADO CHIMICHURRI & STEAK GRILLING TIPS

Every month, the menu at Ember Restaurant changes to reflect the seasons and their culinary creativity, yet one mighty dish has remained a permanent fixture since opening night: their incredible rib-eye steak with avocado chimichurri!

AVOCADO CHIMICHURRI

3 T shallots, minced
1 T lime juice
1 t. red wine vinegar
1 large Hass avocado, diced
½ cup cilantro, minced
¼ cup Italian parsley, minced
1 t. garlic, minced
2 T jalapeño, charred, skinned, seeded, and minced
¼ cup extra virgin olive oil
sea salt and pepper

STEAK

12-14 oz. rib-eye steaks
sea salt
coarsely ground black pepper

RECIPE CONTRIBUTED BY

Brian Collins
Ember Restaurant (p. 157)

AVOCADO CHIMICHURRI

Place the shallots in a mixing bowl; pour the lime juice and vinegar over them. Lightly season with salt and let them macerate for 15 minutes. Add the remaining ingredients and fold them together, making sure the avocados don't get mashed. Season to taste. Cover the bowl with plastic wrap and allow the flavors to meld for about one hour prior to serving.

STEAK TIPS FROM CHEF BRIAN COLLINS OF EMBER RESTAURANT

"To select a nice steak I look for good marbling. Marbling is the subtle presence of fat in most meats, the threads that run between and through the muscle meat. If you are unsure what to look for, simply ask the butcher working behind the counter and they could point out the steaks with the best marbling for you. Since we cut each rib-eye steak at our restaurant by hand, we also take the time to trim off any overabundance of fat from the 'tail' and 'fat cap'. Leaving the right amount of fat in the right places on the steak is important because during the grilling process it will render and become golden-brown, crispy, and delicious.

For the actual cooking of the steak, I believe that a wood fire and embers produce the best flavor. Before building the fire there are a couple of very important things I do to the meat:

1. I always have the steaks at room temperature before cooking. A cold steak cooks less evenly and the fat on the inside does not warm up or melt away like it should (assuming you are cooking the steak rare to medium).

2. I season the steak with sea salt and coarsely ground black pepper. Seasoning an hour ahead of time allows the seasoning to get inside the steak.

For the actual cooking, I make sure that I am grilling the steak over glowing, red-hot embers or coals. You want to cook the meat with intense heat. This searing heat will caramelize the outside of the steak, giving it a nice crust. Depending on the thickness of the steak you will need to adjust the grills' proximity to the coals; the thicker the steak, the closer you want it to the heat. The steak should be turned a few times so that both the coloring and cooking are even."

CARROT CAKE CUPCAKES WITH CREAM CHEESE FROSTING

Spring screams carrots! For a fun presentation, add shavings of rainbow carrots and a sprig of greenery to the tops of these cream cheese frosted cupcakes.

BATTER

2 cups sugar
2 cups flour
4 eggs
½ t. baking soda
2 t. salt
2 t. cinnamon
¼ t. clove
¼ t. nutmeg
1 T vanilla
1 cup canola oil
½ cup buttermilk
3 heaping cups carrots, shredded

CREAM CHEESE FROSTING

6 oz. cream cheese, softened
8 oz. unsalted butter, softened
1 lb. powdered sugar
1 T vanilla
milk (optional)

BATTER

Preheat oven to 350°F. In a standup mixer, mix everything (except the carrots) together until smooth. Add the carrots and mix until incorporated. Line a cupcake tray with cupcake liners; bake for 10–15 minutes. Remove from oven and let cool.

CREAM CHEESE FROSTING

In a standup mixer, whip the cream cheese. Add the butter, cream thoroughly. Slowly add the powdered sugar and vanilla. Whip until smooth and silky. If needed, add a few splashes of milk to achieve the desired consistency.

» Frost the cupcakes once they are cool enough to handle. Garnish with carrot shavings and greenery.

RECIPE CONTRIBUTED BY

Jeremy Davenport
Éclair Bakery (p. 156)

NOT YOUR GRANDMA'S CHERRY PIE

When it comes to wine, according to Chef Alyx, a good rule of thumb is, "If you can't drink it, don't cook with it." Prepare to have your taste buds rocked by this kickass cherry pie!

FILLING

2 cups red wine
8 organic black peppercorns
1 bay leaf
½ cup organic evaporated cane sugar
pinch of salt
4 cups organic cherries
2 T aluminum-free organic cornstarch

PIE CRUST

2½ cups of organic white flour
1 T organic evaporated cane sugar
¾ t. raw Himalayan sea salt
1 cup grass-fed raw cultured butter, chilled
6 T vodka, chilled

FILLING

In a small stainless steel sauce pan, add red wine, peppercorns, and bay leaf. Simmer and reduce wine by half. Remove the bay leaf; add sugar and salt. Reduce on simmer for an additional 5–7 minutes while stirring slowly. Remove peppercorns and let cool to room temperature. (This part of the the recipe can be prepared up to a week before hand.) While that cools, prepare the pie crust.

PIE CRUST

Mix flour, sugar, and salt in a food processor. Add butter; pulse until coarse meal forms. Add chilled vodka one tablespoon at a time; pulse once or twice until dough forms into moist clumps. Gather dough into a ball and divide into two discs. Wrap each disc individually in plastic wrap and chill for 2 hours minimum, optimally 24 hours.

Remove the dough from the refrigerator. Roll out the dough, gently place one dough disc in the bottom and sides of a 9-inch pie dish, and prick all over with a fork.

» Preheat oven to 450°F. Pit and halve the cherries. Add cornstarch and cherries to the red wine reduction; stir gently till thoroughly mixed and coated. Fill into the prepared pie crust. Roll out your other disc and cover the pie. With water, moisten where they meet, then tuck the top crust under the bottom to create a seal—a tuck-and-pinch technique—then flute the edge. Cut slits in a flower shape pattern radiating from the center of the pie to allow steam to escape.

Place pie on a baking sheet in the center of the oven for 10 minutes at 450°F, then reduce to 350°F for an additional 45–55 minutes. You are looking for a nice golden crust.

Genius tip: "Give pies as a gift. Go to a thrift store and get a pie dish—should only cost you a few bucks. That way you don't have to ask for your dish back and your friend can keep it as a keepsake!" says Chef Alyx.

RECIPE CONTRIBUTED BY
Alyx Gille
Good Tides Organic Bistro (p. 160)

HOW TO BUILD THE ULTIMATE CHEESE BOARD

Cheese makes everything better. This may be a personal opinion—but it is also a fact! Trust me, I'm an expert when it comes to cheese boards—my credentials include years of cheesemongering in San Francisco at Mission Cheese.

ACCOUTREMENTS SUGGESTIONS

fresh fruit
local honey
nuts
bread
crackers
charcuterie
mustard
pickled vegetables
mostarda
dried fruit
olives
jam
preserves
marmalades
chutneys

BEFRIEND YOUR LOCAL CHEESEMONGER

Go to your local cheese shop or cheese counter to strike up conversation with your new best friend: the cheesemonger. These turophiles (connoisseurs of cheese) are happy to help. Do not be timid about asking questions—cheesemongers are always eager to unleash glorious cheese knowledge on you. Still feeling intimidated? Don't be. Reality check: cheese is old milk. That's all. There is no need to be intimidated by old milk.

PARAMETERS

It's good to pass on some parameters to the cheesemonger when choosing cheeses: *How many people is this board intended for? Is this cheese board a casual snack, small appetizer, or after-dinner dessert? What is your budget?*

LESS IS MORE

In my opinion, an ideal cheese board has 3–5 cheeses. You want each cheese to be truly memorable and distinct from the others on the board.

MMMMMILK

A good rule of thumb is to have all your milk bases covered: goat, sheep, cow, and even mixed milks. Sometimes cheeses are made with raw milk, while others are made with pasteurized milk. Both are delicious and both are safe for consumption.

AGE IS JUST A NUMBER

"Cheese: milk's leap toward immortality," said Clifton Fadiman. You are going to want to include a range of ages to cover the whole spectrum from young, soft, spreadable, runny, and creamy, to firm, semi-hard, hard, crumbly, and aged.

FLAVOR PROFILES

Now comes the fun part: flavor! Over time you will become familiar with cheeses and their descriptors: sharp, nutty, grassy, bright, briny, sweet, meaty, stinky, pungent, mild, funky, salty, buttery, tangy, barnyardy, etc.

You will quickly learn which flavors are your favorite. Enjoy the cheese journey: familiarize yourself with specific cheese names; learn about the regions, process, and rich cultural history behind each cheese; research the the story behind the cheesemaker (p. 177).

RIND—TO EAT OR NOT TO EAT?

"Should I eat the rind?!"—a question I often heard from panicky people wanting to avoid potential embarrassment in front of a pretentious crowd of cheese eaters. My answer is simple: if you want to. Rinds are always edible—unless they are clearly not edible, e.g. wax or cloth. You will know; use your instinct. Some people love eating the rinds, as they add another depth of unique flavor, while other folks don't care for it. It's totally your personal preference and will vary from cheese to cheese. My two cents: always try the rind to figure it out for yourself.

CUTTING THE CHEESE

Haaaaaaaaa—that joke will never not be funny! Make sure to serve cheese at room temperature. If you plan on slicing, do so right before serving so that the cheese doesn't dry out.

ACCOUTREMENTS

That's a fancy French word for additional items. There are heaps of tasty *accoutrements* out there to accompany your cheese board: fresh fruit, local honey, nuts, bread, crackers, charcuterie, mustard, pickled vegetables, mostarda, dried fruit, olives, jam, preserves, marmalades, and chutneys. When it comes to eating cheese, I'm a total purist. I like to enjoy the cheese all by itself and I use the *accoutrements* as palate cleansers. Once I've tasted the cheese and identified the flavor profile, then I will start to experiment with pairing it with other tasty treats on the board.

PRESENTATION

No one likes to be the first to dig into a cheese flight—unless you are me and have no reservations in getting a cheese party started. Therefore make the presentation inviting. Dedicate one knife per cheese; cut a few wedges, crumbles, and batons of the cheeses. Make the *accoutrements* enticing as well: slice fruit, crack nuts, drizzle honey, toast crostini. Make it beautiful and have fun.

THEMED FLIGHTS

Creating cheese flights that have themes is fun. Try making a flight with all the same milk but with very different ages. Create an all-local cheese plate highlighting your state's cheesemakers. If using imported cheeses, source from the same country. Select cheeses from the same family or the same type so you can compare and contrast flavor profiles. The sky's the limit!

Share your experience with the hashtag:
#slofarmersmarketcookbook

SHORT STORIES

"In 2006, when we opened our doors, Paso was becoming an up-and-coming region at the time. It's really become established these past couple of years—we've even been rated the #1 wine region in the world by Wine Enthusiast in 2013. Things have come a long way, so now it's time for food to get focused in that direction," explains Chef Chris Kobayashi. A true champion of the local, seasonal, farm-to-table movement, Chris does 16 formal menu changes throughout the year, and sometimes tweaks items slightly each week. Additionally, for the past 8 years, he and his fellow farmers have hosted the *Outstanding in the Field* dinners. These open-air feasts connect diners to the local land through farm-to-table dinners—a truly unique celebration and collaboration between local farmers and chefs. Chris is always driven by what is available at the market. "When you understand your ingredients, they dictate what you make. Whatever is seasonally available and abundant is always at it's peak—that is what is going to give you the best dish possible." A man of morals, Chris operates his restaurant organically and sustainably, even all the way down to the chicken bones and onions. "My team and I all feel that we are putting out the best product. It all starts with good ingredients; once you have good ingredients you don't have to do that much to them, just a little technician work and you have a beautiful dish."

BAUTISTA FARMS

MANUEL BAUTISTA

Originally hailing from the Mexican state of Guerrero, Manuel Bautista of Bautista Farms has been farming since the early 80s. "I came from a small town. My dad raised cows and grew corn. In 1983, I started working with one of my cousins growing peas on the Central Coast, and in 1988 I started my own farm." When Manuel first started farming, he only grew squash and cherry tomatoes—now he grows everything under the sun! "In 1988 I started selling at the farmers' market. We started with 2 boxes of squash. Now I grow salad mix, spinach, kale, chard, arugula. I grow three different types of peas: English peas, snap peas, and snow peas. I've got blackberries, raspberries, strawberries. We have tomatoes, onions, yellow beets, red beets, leeks, green beans, carrots, zucchini, yellow crookneck, fava beans, and fennel." Life on his beautiful Arroyo Grande farm in Huasna Valley runs like clockwork. "Mondays, Tuesdays, Thursdays, and Fridays we pick in the fields. On Fridays we pick for five markets—one on Friday, three on Saturday, and one on Sunday. We keep everything in a cooler, and on Monday we start all over again. I have 4–5 guys who help me pick every week." Lucky for us, all of his produce stays within the County; it is sold at farmers' market and directly to restaurants that support the locavore movement. In order to keep up the demand, his wife makes a list each night of what needs to be picked the following day for their markets and local accounts.

Manuel beams with pride over his produce and gushes gratitude for his lifestyle; "I like everything about my job. It's really nice. I get to do so many things each day. I'm really happy with the crew I have right now. I love farming so much! I thank God for giving me the opportunity to farm. I'm really happy and so proud of everything we do." It's no wonder their booth is always bustlin' and chefs specifically mention his farm on their menus; his passion for growing is palpable!

BIG SKY CAFE

GREG HOLT

Chef/Owner Greg Holt has been at Big Sky Cafe for 16 of the 21 years it's been open. Breakfast, lunch, and dinner are served daily with rotating specials and over 20 local wines by the glass. "There is a great energy here, we get to do good food. We are malleable based on the seasons."

WHAT INSPIRES YOU WHEN CREATING SEASONAL DISHES?

All the credit goes to the farmers. I have a small repertoire of what to do with food; it pretty much depends on what my farmers grow. The more they grow, the more I learn. Once you start shopping at the local farmers' markets, you learn what to get, from whom, and when. It's all about following the flow of the farms.

WHAT IS A STAPLE MENU ITEM AT BIG SKY CAFE?

We have a goat cheese salad that we keep on the menu year-round because it is delicious and delightful. Happy Acres Farm has managed to keep the goats producing cheese year-round, and we pair it with whoever has the nicest arugula at the time—Windrose Farms, Rutiz Farms (p. 180), or Bautista Farms (p. 151). If it's late summer, then we pair it with whoever has the most delicious fruit. We just had the last figs of the season—I just cried a little bit. But we will have winter squash coming in soon; as soon as I get beautiful delicata, then we will start putting roasted delicata on that salad.

HOW WOULD YOU DESCRIBE THE CUISINE AT BIG SKY CAFE?

We do good, fresh, real, farm-to-table food. We try to take food that everyone is comfortable with—chicken, fish, pork—and we prepare it in a new, interesting, and health-conscious way.

CAL POLY ORGANIC FARM

The 11-acre Cal Poly Organic Farm's educational emphasis is designed to educate students with hands-on learning in organic and sustainable farming and gardening practices. A faculty director with expertise in some aspect of agriculture guides the coursework related to the farm and is also responsible for the Organic Certification. The farm also has a farm manager, who is a Certified Organic farmer with their own local farm, and who is in the field everyday with students, teaching them the ins-and-outs of all aspects of organic farming practices.

Interview with director Professor David Headrick, Ph.D.; photo of Farm Manager Jerry Mahoney.

WHAT IS THE VISION OF THE CAL POLY ORGANIC FARM PROGRAM?

The vision is consistent with Cal Poly's teaching style—the "learn by doing" approach. It is what students come here for, it is what they appreciate; so it's no surprise that, when they develop a program like the organic farm, a major focus is experiential learning. The organic farm will always be a teaching tool. It is also another facet of our plant production department that includes fruit, flowers, and other crops—we have all of this activity under one roof. It's great for the students to see just how much goes into making the food we eat and the plants we use to beautify our lives.

WHAT CROPS DO YOU GROW?

We grow a large variety so that students can observe the different crop types and how they are grown, harvested, and readied for market. We also make our very own transplants for many of our vegetables and herbs.

CHEF JENSEN LORENZEN

FORMERLY OF THE CASS HOUSE INN & RESTAURANT

PHOTOS BY KEN KIENOW.

The Cass House Inn & Restaurant holds a very special place in my heart. During the last few months of operation, my husband and I were lucky enough to dine at this intimate establishment—regarded by some as "The French Laundry of the Central Coast." After enjoying several courses and wine in the warm, dimly lit dining room, we strolled down to the beach swingsets just a block away. It was here that my husband popped *the question*. I will cherish the memory of this meal and moment forever. I reached out to Chef Jensen Lorenzen to tell him about my lovely experience. "I am glad that we were a part of such a memorable evening. The memories we create for people are our lifeblood, and not unlike those memories, Grace (his wife) and I will also always have the memories of the special people we served." Known for his extravagant tasting menus highlighting the true *terroir* of the Central Coast, Jensen foraged and sourced only the freshest seasonal produce and herbs—many of which were grown biodynamically by the cooks in the inn's garden. "I like that, as a cook, you learn to transform inedible raw ingredients, into delicious meals [and] you are trained to make almost anything taste good. There is really no good reason for it, other than it makes people happy. Doing something exclusively because it makes people happy is just the most amazing thing to me. The added bonus is that food brings people together. I can't imagine anything more rewarding than sitting around eating and drinking wine with friends and family." Jensen is now cooking privately for small groups, writing, teaching, and consulting. For his latest, find him at *www.jensenlorenzen.com*.

DOMINGO FARMS
DOMINGO FAMILY

Rudy Domingo has been farming his whole life. "It's a family business. I grew up on a farm, on the same property that we now farm. We own 150 acres—we lease out a lot of it, we farm on about 35 acres—and grow vegetables, herbs, and cut flowers."

I'VE ALWAYS ADMIRED YOUR BEAUTIFUL BOOTH, WHAT DO YOU GROW AND WHY?

We grow what does well on the Central Coast. Year-round we grow green garlic, dandelion, cilantro, Tuscan kale, Russian kale, beets, leeks, radish, carrots. In the summertime we add basil, tomatoes, and peppers. In the winter we grow winter bulbs: tulips, irises, ranunculus, sweet peas. In the spring and summer we like to grow sunflowers and tuberoses. Personally, I like the tuberoses! They are so fragrant: they just smell up the whole place! They catch everybody's nose and their scent fills up Higuera Street. We used to grow about 20 different types of flowers but because of the way the economy is, people are going to eat before they buy flowers.

WHAT DO YOU ENJOY ABOUT SELLING AT THE LOCAL MARKETS?

You develop customers and friends; people come back every week at the market. I would never have another person work the out-of-town markets for us—it's a family thing. Other farms hire people to drive out here to sell their products. You are never going to see the faces of the farmers, so there is not that personal connection. We are only 10 minutes away and anyone is welcome to come to our farm to visit and see how we do things. I'm honest about my farming practices—although we are not Certified Organic, we don't use pesticides of any type.

ÉCLAIR BAKERY

JEREMY DAVENPORT

Every village needs a bakery, and every bakery needs a Jeremy Davenport. He is kind, generous, gregarious—in other words, just the type of person you want to see when grabbing a delicious baked good. You instantly feel you've always been lifelong friends with him, even if it's your first time meeting him.

CAN YOU TELL ME ABOUT YOUR BELIEFS ON MENTORSHIP?

I've always wanted to help people in the community because I've been shown a lot of help. A lot of people have opened up themselves and their doors to me, so I'd like to pass that on to others that are passionate about learning and baking. In fact, our whole bread program started because Kirsten (p. 162) would put doughs together in the evening and I would come in during the morning and bake them off; that's how she got her start. Kelli (p. 186) approached me because she wanted to sell baked treats at farmers' market and was looking to rent space from me. At the beginning we did trade; she would do a little work for me and would use my space in the off hours.

WHAT IS YOUR FAVORITE SEASON TO BAKE IN?

In the summer I really like using a lot of fresh berries (p. 45) and I love making fruit tarts (p. 77). I'll go to the farmers' market and get an assortment of berries [and] whatever I make with them sells immediately. Winter is one of my favorite times to bake too because it's a "comfort food" time of year. I like doing quick breads, cookies, and pumpkin-everything overload!

WHAT'S IT LIKE TO BE AN INTEGRAL PART OF CHARMING DOWNTOWN ARROYO GRANDE?

I love the relationships that I've formed with customers and employees. Nobody comes into the bakery grumpy. Everyone is stoked, everyone gets that immediate satisfaction. I get to talk to people, find out about their day, where they are from. I really value that part of it.

EMBER RESTAURANT

BRIAN COLLINS

The moment you enter Ember, you instantly feel the warmth of the space: the fire, the food, the ambiance—everything about the environment is incredibly inviting. The massive turquoise-tiled pizza oven mesmerizes you as flames tickle the perfect amount of char on their delicious dishes sitting in cast-iron skillets and on pizza paddles. The beautiful build-out boasts rustic barnyard wood paneling, structural high beams, soft glowing string lights, and a sleek copper bar serving up craft beer and a well-curated wine list. Wonderful wafts of authentic hand-crafted food fill the air: grilled rib-eye steak with garlic confit and avocado chimichurri (p. 139), wood-fired squid with cannellini beans, pan-roasted sea scallops with fried green tomatoes, and at the center of it all is Chef/Owner Brian Collins in his big white coat—cool, calm, and collected. Shaking hands with friends and smiling at guests from across the room, Brian ensures that everyone is taken care of and everyone feels connected to the metaphorical communal table. "I think that with fire and food, it connects you to your inner caveman. Up until 150 years ago we only cooked with fire and coals; there are flavors to be found there with that intense heat." Ember celebrates this to its fullest. The majority of the ever-changing menu items are baked in the wood-fired oven or grilled over open flames. With years of experience at Chez Panisse in Berkeley and Full of Life Flatbread in Los Alamos, it was only a matter a time before the A.G. native opened up his very own restaurant. Ember's future burns bright, as they were featured in the *New York Times* as a must-visit destination in SLO County. "We are so grateful that people love what we are doing!"

ESTHER'S GARDEN

ESTHER RIGONI

Farmer Esther Rigoni of Arroyo Grande grows the most beautiful bell peppers and flowers. She frequents many markets throughout the week: Morro Bay (Thursdays), SLO (Thursdays), Cambria (Fridays), SLO (Saturdays), and Arroyo Grande (Saturdays). You can't miss her colorful booth!

WHAT GOT YOU INTERESTED IN FLOWER FARMING?

That's an easy one! Years ago when I was still in High School, my family and I went to Butchart Gardens in Victoria, Canada. Those gardens are really something else! I saw that and I thought, "I will grow flowers some day"—and I did! I started out with little Statice bouquets; they are pretty little dried flowers. I've grown every dried everlasting flower there ever was. All of them. That is how I started. I started with flowers and sweet corn.

WHY DO YOU DIVERSIFY YOUR CROPS AND WHAT ARE YOU KNOWN FOR?

I've always struggled with that. You can have a table full of only peas or a table full of ten different things, and you would probably make the same amount of money. But it just gets boring only producing one crop! I always want to try something new. I always tend to grow flowers, onions, squash, shallots, beans, and lots of peppers. I'm known for my peppers, I do all the different colors.

WHAT DO YOU LOVE ABOUT YOUR JOB?

The sunsets! Every night I'm out there by myself and my sweet yellow lab Chelsea. Sometimes it can be lonely, but every time I see that sunset I think, "Wow! I'm so lucky to see these beautiful sunsets!"

FOREMOST WINE CO.

JULIE SIMON

"In 2005 I was studying law in Bordeaux. I wanted to take a break, travel, and figure out exactly what I wanted to do. I figured I'd come out to California in the summer to stay with my aunt and uncle who produce olive oil in Templeton (Olea Farms), learn English, get a part-time job, and then move back to France—but then I never moved back. Ha!" says Julie Simon, Chef of Foremost Wine Co. In her early teens her mother bought a brasserie in the southwest of France. From an early age Julie would help out by bartending and cooking; it was here that she discovered she had a knack for the culinary world. During her summer-stint turned 10-year stay, Julie has done a lot. She has been the Sous Chef at both Windows on the Water and The Park, the Head Chef at Thomas Hill Organics (p. 188), and is now the Executive Chef of Foremost Wine Co. At age 28 she is making quite the name and impressive career for herself!

Foremost features an eclectic menu featuring unique seasonal burrata dishes made with their own pickles and preserves, rotating daily selections of cheeses and in-house cured charcuterie, and small and large plates highlighting local produce, dairy, and meat. "We wanted to make food that was wine-friendly. You know the saying *what grows together, goes together?* I believe that is very true and so I'm trying not to mimic just one cuisine, but all cultures that cook wine-friendly food." Their menus even have a translucent tracing-paper overlay that highlights suggested wine pairings for each dish. "I want people to order many different and flavorful plates to share amongst their friends and family."

Central Coast native Chef Alyx Gille of Good Tides Organic Bistro is the superstar of SLO County farmers' markets! Every delicious ingredient that goes into her organic baked goods, soups, salads, and fermented larder staples is thoughtfully sourced and seasonally driven; every item is made from scratch with a whole lotta heart. "My family and I have always eaten this way—nothing from a box, bag, jar, or can!" She sources everything from her farmer friends at the markets. "I don't know what I'm going to sell at Saturday's market until I've shopped at Thursday's market. It's whatever I can get my hands on; we don't ever have a set menu which allows me a lot of creative freedom."

Growing up, her family significantly shaped her philosophy on cooking. "My German grandmother taught me how to make bratwurst and sauerkraut. We are a food family, we always have been. Nobody ever wanted to come to my house after school for snacks. Haha! We had blue corn tortilla chips and guacamole. My sandwiches at lunch would be sprouts, avocado, and Muenster cheese on dark rye bread."

Alyx has done it all. She attended culinary school in San Francisco, ran her own personal chef business in Ireland for 7 years, operated Good Tides Coffee House for 2 years and Good Tides Organic Bistro restaurant for 3 years (both in Los Osos). Now she focuses her efforts on selling at farmers' markets and on catering. "I get to create exactly what I want, using the exact ingredients that I want, then I get to hand it to people. I love it! My hope is that people can taste my food and realize how much better it is—simple and seasonal."

GOOD TIDES ORGANIC BISTRO

ALYX GILLE

JULIA'S JUICES

JULIA GOMEZ

Julia Gomez of Julia's Juices started juicing in April 2012 while working at her sister's farm when she started to notice the positive benefits of raw juice on her health. While working at Bautista Farms (p. 151), Julia and her husband Javier of Red Barn Farms (p. 175) moved into a small house on a farm right next door, which allowed Javier to grow his own produce.

WHAT INSPIRED YOU TO START SELLING FARM FRESH JUICE?

One of the managers of the San Luis Obispo markets told us we had to do something unique in order to be able to sell at market—so we decided to juice! Juicing was a way to condense everything that was being grown on the farm and use it in a way that would generate profit and growth. Now we sell both our juice and our produce at many markets throughout SLO County.

CAN YOU WALK ME THROUGH THE FIELD-TO-PITCHER PROCESS?

We start on the farm the day before, picking all the produce that is needed for the next day; everything gets washed, sorted, and loaded into our car. The next day, I wake up early to head to the juice bar in Grover Beach. We wash all the produce again and prep everything to be put through our extractors. Since we make such large quantities, we make all the juices separately, then I mix the combinations together. We clean up the kitchen and load up to go to the markets. Any leftover fibers or vegetable matter gets taken back to the farm to feed the animals.

WHAT'S THE DIFFERENCE BETWEEN RAW JUICE AND PASTEURIZED JUICE?

Pasteurization helps to kill any bacteria that may be in raw juices; however, pasteurization also breaks down enzymes and kills good nutrients. We do not bottle our juices, which allows them to be kept raw. Arguably, raw juices are more beneficial to your system because they have not lost any enzymes nor nutrients.

LITTLE RED HEN BREAD

KIRSTEN FINBERG

Kirsten Finberg of Little Red Hen Bread is a pint-sized ball of energy with a go-getter attitude. After spending a few years running the bread program at Éclair Bakery (p. 156) and attending a weeklong bread baking class at the San Francisco Baking Institute, she was itching to go out on her own. On her walks to the bakery, she would always pass the big brick oven at Rooster Creek Tavern. One day she approached the owner about using the oven in the off-hours. He agreed, so she would go between 1 a.m. and 8 a.m. to bake her bread. "During their operation hours their oven was set to pizza temperature which is about 715°F. The brick oven retains heat and it drops during the night—I bake bread at 550°F, so essentially that heat wasn't getting used anyways. I never turned on the gas, I was just using the residual heat, so it worked out great! It was perfect! They were absolutely amazing to let me use it." Passed in January 2013 in California, Cottage Food Law allows certain foods to be prepared at private home kitchens to be sold at farmers' markets, grocers, and retail shops. Kirsten took full advantage of this by commissioning an amazing outdoor oven at her home in the Arroyo Grande Village. You can find her beautiful loaves—seeded whole wheat sourdough, focaccia, olive and sea salt, blue cheese sourdough (p. 92), and baguettes—at markets throughout the week and at Rutiz's farm stand on Fridays (p. 180).

LOS OSOS VALLEY ORGANIC FARM

JIM TERRICK

"I'm a Certified Organic grower. I believe in it. You have to believe it because often times the bottom line doesn't show; you have to believe in it enough to make the sacrifices," says Jim Terrick of Los Osos Valley Organic Farm. Jim sells at market (Baywood on Mondays and SLO on Saturdays) and he runs an amazing Certified Organic CSA box program.

WHAT ORGANIC FARMING PRACTICES DO YOU FOLLOW?

Anything we put on the soil or plants has to come from a living or once-living source with a minimum amount of processing. Now, why is this good? It promotes a balanced microbial life in the soil. We add compost or cover crop (known as a green manure) which adds carbon to the soil. Building up carbon creates more microbial diversity and strong fertility. That microbial action breaks down minerals and complex woody material (straw). High organic soils retain moisture better, require less water, grow plants better, and provide a great balance of air, water, and soil in a soil profile.

WHY IS FARMING ORGANICALLY IMPORTANT TO YOU PERSONALLY?

I think we have lost our way. We are trying to dominate nature, but we can do things pretty successfully with the gifts we are given. When we start monkeying around using pesticides, even organic pesticides, we disrupt balance. If your soil is right, you will have almost no insect problems and very few fungal problems. With really good high-quality soil, high organic matter, high microbial life, you just don't have these problems. It happens over and over again—insects build up resistance to insecticide. It's a fight, it's a battle, so I like to enlist nature's help.

LUNA RED RESTAURANT·BAR

SHAUN BEHRENS

"I grew up cooking with my grandmother on her farm in the summers in Idaho. My grandmother and grandfather had a sustainable farm. She was an incredible homemaker—she had her own garden, she used scraps for her chickens, she composted. My grandfather went out to work the fields. They sold beef, alfalfa, and corn. Growing up that meant that the men would work the fields and set the irrigation, and the women would stay inside the house. Well, I didn't know that, ha. I just didn't want to go out in the field to do manual labor, so I stayed in the kitchen with my grandmother! I liked cooking from a very young age," reminisces Chef Shaun Behrens of Luna Red. After culinary school he moved to Portland to work under Greg Higgins—who is essentially the Alice Waters of Oregon. "His restaurant, Higgins, is completely farm-to-table. He cures all his own charcuterie, does an amazing pickle program, makes in-house pastas, and basically cooks everything from scratch. I started to remember cooking with my grandmother, and it came full circle for me. I had this response that I had to do that, I felt I had this responsibility in me—as chefs it's our mission to cook responsibly and ethically for people. We are professionals. People trust us." Shaun was the Executive Chef at Robin's (p. 179) in Cambria before owners Shanny (p. 178) and Robin (p. 171) conceptualized and opened Luna Red. "Our cuisine is very unique, it's latin-inspired dining with lots of small shareable tapas. I don't know one table that doesn't share their food here! We have evolved to offer scratch-cooking food using local sources, a huge cocktail program, and an award-winning wine list."

MAMA'S MEATBALL
NICOLA ALLEGRETTA

Nicola Allegretta has done it all—chef, farmer, restaurant consultant, menu developer, opened several restaurants, started a catering company—and most importantly, he has raised a family. Mama's Meatball is a family business at it's core: his Mama makes the desserts and her mind-melting marinara sauce, his Dad sells at farmers' market, his brothers Cosimo and Luca cook behind the line in the kitchen, and his wife Jackeline coordinates the catering and event planning. During my time at Cal Poly, I was a server at his restaurant and they truly treated me like *famiglia*!

WHAT WAS YOUR CHILDHOOD LIKE GROWING UP IN ITALY?

I grew up on a farm when I was a kid. I really liked that quiet atmosphere in nature. I'm Italian but my family moved to Germany for work. They leased a piece of property and they farmed the land, growing vegetables and raising livestock—rabbits, goats, chickens. Then they moved back to Italy and, in order to make a living, my dad worked on a ship for a few years, but my mom needed help raising my brothers and I. When my dad returned my parents bought a piece of property in Italy. At the time there was a good profit in flower farming, so my family invested in some greenhouses and grew cut flowers. But once Italy switched their currency from the Lira to the Euro people could not afford to buy flowers anymore, so we decided to grow vegetables again.

WHEN DID YOU COME TO THE UNITED STATES?

I worked at the Italian restaurant in the Epcot Center at Walt Disney World in Orlando, Florida as the Kitchen Manager. We settled in San Luis Obispo in 2004. I started Mama's Meatball with my family in 2006, which features casual, authentic Italian cuisine using the finest and freshest locally grown ingredients!

MAMA'S PRESERVES

LORI HEAL

Born and raised in SLO, Lori Heal of Mama's Preserves is a fourth-generation resident. She comes from a lineage of dairymen and cattlemen, and is continuing the family legacy herself by farming fruits, veggies, and making preserves. As a mother of four boys, she radiates kindness and warmth. Her down-to-earth, nurturing personality shines when she is sampling and you can really taste the love she puts into every jar.

HOW LONG HAVE YOU BEEN INVOLVED WITH FARMING, MARKETS, AND JAMMING?

I've been farming and going to farmers' markets for 30 years, and I've been doing jam for about 15 years. I used to sell only the fruits as-is, but then I started canning. I got into jamming because I had extra raspberries and olallieberries and I didn't want to waste them. I started playing around, and my mom and family encouraged me to do something with the jams. So I did! My husband built me a beautiful certified kitchen which is on our property out in Corbett Canyon.

HOW DID THE FIRST MARKET GO?

Ha! I show up with a tray of sugar snap peas and a big platter of dip. People never even knew about snap peas; I would have them grab a pea and dip it into some ranch, and they absolutely fell in love with it. We starting bringing sugar snap peas, then snow peas, then blueberries, and from there we just grew!

WHAT DO YOU LOVE ABOUT FARMERS' MARKET?

I get so filled by people—the compliments, the hugs, the kisses. I've watched so many little ones grow up to be adults, and now they are having kids—I love it!

MEZE WINE BAR & BISTRO

LISA & JOHN SCHILTZ

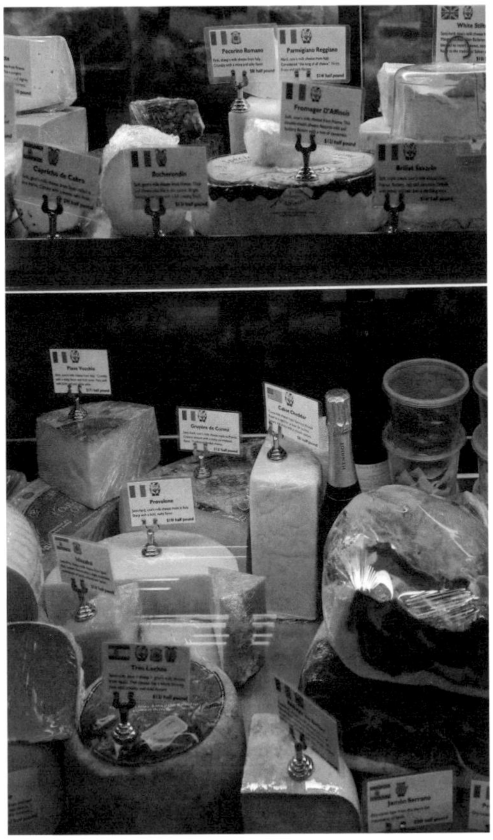

Hailing from the Bay Area, Lisa and John both ditched their day jobs in high-tech to pursue their true passion: food and wine! Lisa has always been a huge foodie—she has taken courses with master chefs and even private lessons with farm-to-table goddess Alice Waters. John became an assistant winemaker and attended the French Culinary Institute to become a certified sommelier. Then the search to acquire a restaurant was on. "Meze was exactly what we wanted—we liked the open space and the industrial, urban feel. The existing menu was really good, too. We weren't crazy about the existing wine program but that was okay because we knew that we could make the changes. John handles the beer and wine program and has completely revamped it." Lisa has also put her own twist on the pre-existing menu by tweaking some of the recipes and adding her own. She creates a new *tartine du jour* every week and rotates soups based on the seasons: summer corn bisque, roasted tomato and garlic soup, artichoke and lemon soup, mushroom soup, to name a few. "It's not about eating, dining, and leaving, it's about making every meal an occasion. Whether you are chilling with friends or grabbing a drink after work with colleagues, it's about turning that into something more. It's about taking the time to enjoy the company and the wine, and having great food that compliments both."

MT. OLIVE ORGANIC FARM

NG FAMILY

PHOTOS BY SHEA SOMMA.

Started by 3 Christian families in the early 90s, Mt. Olive Organic Farm strives to be as pure as possible when cultivating their 150 acres in Paso Robles. Every major decision is made by the group—and no matter what your role is on the farm, everyone has the chance to garden and do outside field work.

WHY DO YOU BELIEVE IN ORGANIC FARMING?

According to the Beginning, in God's First Creation, there were no chemicals, no pesticides, no herbicides, no synthetic fertilizers. Therefore all our compost, produce, and products at Mt. Olive are Certified Organic. That's what we are trying to bring to people—the best of health and God's First Creation.

WHAT ARE YOUR ORGANIC FARMING PRACTICES?

To manage an organic farm, compost is the basic fertilizer. We have small piles of compost that we flip manually and large piles that are flipped by a machine. When the compost is ready we don't put it directly in our soil; first we feed it to our earth worms. Then we collect the earthworm castings—it makes for the best compost and the best fertilizer in the world! We don't pull anything completely out—absolutely no uprooting. Instead we just cut the grass low so that we can save the microorganisms in the soil—when you pull out weeds it dries up the soil and harms the beneficial little critters inside, so we just trim the weeds short to the ground.

WHAT ARE SOME SUSTAINABLE PRACTICES YOU INCORPORATE?

About 10 years ago is when we starting adding other products: jam, dehydrated fruit, nuts—we don't let anything go to waste. If we can't sell it or eat it ourselves we make it into juice, jam, or dried fruit. If we can't process it then our animals eat the remainder! We have cattle, pigs, goats, chickens, piglets, and we even have a little petting zoo next to our cafe and store!

NEGRANTI CREAMERY

ALEXIS NEGRANTI

PHOTOS BY KELSEA HOLDER | KELSEAHOLDER.COM

When I asked Alexis Negranti to share some quotes that keep her inspired, she rapidly fired off a few without any hesitation: "Throw caution to the wind. Just go for it. Say yes and figure it out later. Learn by doing. Fake it 'til you make it. My advice is: Don't be scared. If you don't do something you are really passionate about, you will regret it. A lot of people never try because they are scared. Scared of what? Failure? If you fail, who cares? At least you tried." Nearly 3 years ago, Alexis was the very first interview I conducted for this cookbook and these were the exact words I needed to hear.

The story goes: one day Alexis decided she wanted to start a sheep dairy and make sheep's milk ice cream. Little details like having never milked a sheep in her life and never once making homemade ice cream didn't phase her one bit. Alexis is a dreamer and a do-er, a one-two punch that allows her to excel at anything she puts her mind to. One month later she and her husband (who at the time was unsure if you could even milk sheep!) returned home with a flock of sheep and she started churning out delicious pints. "At the time I started I was the only sheep's milk ice creamery in the nation. The milk is really rare and precious; sheep produce such little milk, about half a gallon a day, as opposed to a goat that produces 3–5 gallons a day or a cow that produces 10 gallons a day." Her teat-to-table operation—brilliantly coined by her clever husband Wade—was a success from the beginning. "I had no idea of what I was getting myself into when I started my company. I feel very fortunate and lucky. I'm so thankful that people enjoy the product and that I enjoy making it."

NOVO RESTAURANT & LOUNGE

BEN RICHARDSON

Chef Ben Richardson has been with Novo since its inception in 2003. While the restaurant was under construction, he did a lot of menu development at Robin's Restaurant (p. 179) in Cambria—the sister restaurant to both Novo and Luna Red (p. 164). He worked at Novo for 5 years before taking some time off to co-found a local catering company (Two Cooks Catering) and teach at Cuesta College's culinary program. In 2013, he rejoined the restaurant as the Executive Chef.

WHEN DID YOU KNOW YOU WANTED TO BE A CHEF?

I always had a passion for food; even as a young kid I remember watching the PBS show Great Chefs!

HOW HAS NOVO EVOLVED?

When we first opened, it was very tapas-driven with smaller plates, similar to what Luna Red is now, but different in that we have always emphasized curries rather than Spanish-influenced cuisine. I did have freedom to do whatever we wanted to do. That was always the beauty of this restaurant—there were no restrictions to regional cuisine, so we could go wherever we wanted. That's always been the attractive thing for me. Robin (p. 171) and I clicked right away because of our philosophies and thoughts about local produce and seasonality.

WHY IS COOKING SEASONALLY IMPORTANT TO YOU?

Supporting local farmers is very important to us. The quality that we get is superior, hands down. Because of where we are on the Central Coast the growing seasons are very forgiving, so we can count on consistency and quality from our amazing farmers.

NOVO RESTAURANT & LOUNGE

ROBIN COVEY

"Shanny and I had a dream of owning a restaurant together and the opportunity presented itself, so we opened Robin's Restaurant in 1985, preceded by our health foods store, called The Robin's Nest, that we opened in 1980," says Robin Covey. He and Shanny (p. 178) co-own three of the most well-known, high-volume, farm-to-table restaurants in the County: Robin's Restaurant in Cambria (p. 179), housed in a beautiful historic adobe home; Luna Red (p. 164), with it's expansive yet intimate patio backed up the the San Luis Obispo Mission; and Novo Restaurant with it's award-winning late-night creekside dining. "Novo carries a bit of Robin's dishes, the menu started as a tapas restaurant but as time went on, we put on more large plates. Novo's menu was created to reach all the demographics—you can go have a salad and a glass of wine, or you can have a rib eye steak. My whole theory on restaurants is to provide something for everyone. I like user-friendly restaurants that are accommodating and offer fresh and exciting food." Due to its popularity and large seating capacity, produce must be brought once (sometimes twice) daily by full-time Market Buyer Matt Kubat, who sources produce for all 3 restaurants. Some of their prefered vendors include: Bautista Farms (p. 151), Cal Poly Organic Farm (p. 153), Domingo Farms (p.155), Esther's Garden (p.158), Pepper Creek Family Farms (p. 174), Mama's Preserves (p. 166), Red Barn Farms (p. 175), and SLO Grown Produce (p. 184). "We've been going to the farmers' market in SLO since 1980—every single week for the past 35 years! Supporting our farmers allows us to create local, wholesome, global cuisine at all 3 iconic restaurants."

OLD SLO BBQ

MATT PEARCE

WHEN WAS THE FIRST TIME YOU HAD SANTA-MARIA STYLE BARBEQUE?

It was at a friend's family's barbeque. I was blown away by how good and different it was—I couldn't believe that I had lived in SLO for almost a decade and I had never experienced Santa Maria-style barbeque! Immediately my mind went spinning—we need to market the seasoning so that people can experience it too! But, come to find out, there is no one thing that makes it Santa Maria-style. I love being able to talk to our customers about how Santa Maria-style barbeque is integrated with the culture of San Luis Obispo, and the families that have been here so long, and the history of the Mexican cowboys, and the Portuguese influence from the Central Valley—all of these things are what make Santa Maria-style barbeque what it is today. The methods, the techniques, and the very simple ingredients that go into the finished product are what make this style of barbeque truly unique.

HOW DID YOU TRANSITION FROM A CATERING COMPANY TO A RESTAURANT?

I'm a Cal Poly Civil & Structural Engineer by trade, and I work out at Diablo Canyon, but I was looking for a creative outlet outside of work. I started catering on the weekends in 2010 with some old family recipes—not my family, but a few of my good friends' families'—and it just took off immediately. We started attending farmers' markets in Avila and Grover to promote our catering company, but what happened is I ended up liking the markets more than I liked the catering! It was more personable; I liked being able to connect with customers on a personal level on a regular basis rather than someone's point of contact for one day. We opened our 380-square foot kitchen in 2012, and it was an immediate hit. You would have thought we had our BBQ bases covered in SLO, but we didn't. There was still room for variety, and no one was doing what I was doing. Since opening we have been more successful every day!

Take a drive down Orcutt Road heading toward Edna Valley and you will see the Baileyana Tasting Room—the quaint, iconic yellow schoolhouse. Across the road from the schoolhouse there is a parcel of land with happy cows, plump pigs, and grazing sheep. These fine animals belong to Jordin and Pete Cramer of PC Cattle Co. "We really appreciate the loyalty of our customers; we just go to the one farmers' market on Saturday morning in San Luis and our customer base consists of people that come back every week. We appreciate their loyalty and their desire to support local agriculture. The support of our customers definitely enables myself, my wife, and our baby Hazel to continue ranching." As a firm believer in sustainable husbandry practices, Pete utilizes the feed sources that are available to him within the SLOcal community. Beer distiller grains from Tap It Brewery, leftover Baba Foods Mediterranean dip samples from market, and bread ends from Lincoln Deli are given to his pigs. Their sheep graze on grass between golf course greens—an eco-friendly lawn mower service where everybody wins! They also lease acreage on different local ranches for their cattle. "We have a set of British White cattle mother cows as our base herd and we try to pick bulls that will be thrifty and energy-efficient." To sample their product, order the "THO burger" from Thomas Hill Organics (p. 188) or Sidecar SLO's burger!

PEPPER CREEK FAMILY FARMS

BOYD FAMILY

"We used to have a house in the village of Arroyo Grande. My grandpa found a listing for a direct house-to-house swap for some farm land out in Huasna Valley. The couple that lived out there was getting older, wanted to travel, and didn't want to take care of the land anymore. My grandparents and parents decided to go in on it together; they just paid the difference which was hardly anything since the couple had been there for so many years—it was ridiculously cheap! At the time my mom was more of a stay-at-home mom, but she was also a florist. She did a lot of flowers for weddings but I don't know what made her want a farm exactly," chuckles Jessica Newell, Diane's daughter. Pepper Creek Family Farms is now run by Diane, her daughter Jessica, and two of her sons, Eric and Morgan, along with Jessica's husband Richard, their son Griffin, and Eric's wife Sara. Previous to the Boyds, the elderly couple used it for cattle and to raise chickens, before house-swapping their country life for village life. Once the Boyds took it over, they kept it as a cattle ranch for 10 years before transitioning it into a produce farm. "We are in this great microclimate, we basically grow anything that can grow in California. We grow lots of row crops: beets, radish, carrots, fava beans, squashes, melons, corn, and dry-farmed tomatoes. We have orchards of citrus, avocados, figs, mulberries, apples, and stone fruit trees. We have a massive hydroponic system in our greenhouses for our living greens, lettuces, basil, and arugula." Many Central Coast restaurants love Pepper Creek's produce: Ember (p. 157), Foremost Wine Co. (p. 159), Luna Red (p. 164), Novo Restaurant (p. 168–169) and Robin's Restaurant (p. 178–179), to name a few. Now, the farm is experiencing a new chapter. Brothers Eric and Morgan are both U.S. Army combat veterans, and along with their family, they are in the process of establishing a training center on their farm for fellow veterans to work in sustainable agriculture in partnership with Cal Poly State University. Stay tuned for big developments in their new venture in 2016 and beyond!

"*Hola mija*, how are you?" was the greeting that immediately tugged at my heartstrings the first time I met Javier Magaña of Red Barn Farms. Stemming from two contracted words "*mi*" (my) and "*hija*" (daughter), everyone on my Mom's side of the family used the term of endearment growing up. It wasn't restricted just to parents either—grandparents, aunts, uncles, cousins, close friends, anyone really—would call you *mija* (or the male counterpart *mijo*). It was a way to signify you were part of the tribe. And with that one little magical word, I instantly felt bonded to Javier and his pesticide-free produce!

RED BARN FARMS

JAVIER MAGAÑA

WHAT INSPIRED YOU TO FARM?

I got interested in farming because of the juicing. I had a problem with my liver; I had gallstones and I had to go to the doctor many times. My wife Julia of Julia's Juices (p. 161), started making juice for us and after that, I never went back to the doctor. You know, there are a lot of people sick with cancer, and a lot of farmers using a lot of pesticides...we just wanted to live better and help others live better.

CAN YOU TELL ME ABOUT YOUR FARMING PRACTICES?

We pick everything on the day we bring it to the markets. We don't put anything in coolers. Everything you see on our table was picked less than 5 hours ago. It's really the freshest you can get!

WHAT IS THE MOST SATISFYING?

When I plant my seeds and two weeks later I see plants coming up— this makes me very happy! I like my chickens, pigs, and goats. We feed all our leftovers to the animals, which also makes me feel good.

RIGHETTI RANCH

RIGHETTI FAMILY

Interview with Dave Righetti.

CAN YOU TELL ME ABOUT YOUR FAMILY'S HISTORY?

My great-grandfather is originally from Switzerland. He and two other brothers came from Switzerland; they immigrated around South America and came to the West Coast. One stayed in Cayucos, one settled in SLO, and the other settled in Santa Maria. My great-grandfather bought this ranch land and started his dairy operation in 1890.

HOW HAS THE RANCH EVOLVED OVER THE GENERATIONS?

Righetti Ranch was a cow dairy up until World War II, then they switched over from dairy, milk, and cheese to beef cattle. In the late 60s my Dad, Ernest Righetti (who lived a full life to the spritely age of 97) built a large reservoir on the ranch and started planting avocados. His original intent was to have irrigated pastures so he could increase his beef operation, but a Cal Poly professor convinced him to plant avocados. When you irrigate land you can get triple the amount of forage from it. He had 4 young children at the time and wanted to add value to the ranch so the reservoir was built in '66 (which at the time was the largest privately-owned reservoir in SLO County), and in '67 he planted the first commercial black avocados on 7 acres. In '68 he planted another 13 acres and we've been planting every year or two since then. We now have 225 acres of avocados!

YOU ARE SURROUNDED BY WINERIES, DID YOUR FAMILY EVER CONSIDER PLANTING GRAPES?

My Dad resisted planting grapes for many years because he didn't want to support the alcohol industry. Times were different back then—to put it into perspective: in his mind planting grapes was akin to planting tobacco. For him it was an important moral choice, so he chose avocados. Many years later his opinion and mentality shifted, and we planted 55 acres of wine grapes in 2006-2007.

RINCONADA DAIRY

CHRISTINE & JIM MAGUIRE

"I've always been interested in food; my husband Jim and I had been growing most of our own food and raising chickens for years. One day a friend gave me a goat—some friend! Ha!" said Christine of Rinconada Dairy, playfully rolling her eyes. "It was really the beginning of the end; I really enjoyed milking them and working with them. I started to seriously look into it: there were quite a few really good goat cheesemakers in this country in the late 90s, but sheep's milk and cheese were almost non-existent." Once she decided to pursue cheesemaking, she and Jim moved out to a beautiful ranch in Santa Margarita. "I had no formal training in cheesemaking. I took a class at Cal Poly back before they had farmstead cheese courses—now part of the curriculum is for students to come out here to Rinconada Dairy to see what a real farmstead creamery is like. That's been fun!" The first cheese she made, and the only cheese she made for a few years, was Pozo Tomme—a 100% raw sheep's milk cheese based loosely on Spanish Manchego cheese. "Then I wanted to create a cheese that was closer to a flavor profile of English farmhouse cheese, so I created La Panza Gold. That wheel is the most difficult to make because there are many steps in its process to develop acidity, but it's the favorite of most people, local restaurants, and even won 1st class in it's category at the American Cheese Society." After that she became interested in making mixed milk cheeses, "I made Chaparral, which is about two thirds sheep's milk and one third goat's milk—it's very simple and similar to an Italian farmhouse cheese." Her operation continued to expand and she found herself with an overabundance of goat's milk, which lead her to create Carrizo. "It's a good aged goat's milk cheese. Our goats are Nubians because they have the highest butterfat content in their milk; it's the sweetest milk and they are a really beautiful breed." The duo also raises 100 meat chickens every week and tend to 50 egg layers and whey-fed pigs. "Jim is the one that milks at 5 in the morning before he steps into a phone booth and turns into a Super Attorney and goes to work. He is amazing!"

ROBIN'S RESTAURANT

SHANNY COVEY

"The experience at Robin's is one of comfort. It's welcoming. It's cozy. It feels like home. We've had the blessing of being established for 30 years," beams Shanny Covey. She and Robin (p. 171) co-own three of the most well-known, high-volume, farm-to-table restaurants in the County: Robin's Restaurant in Cambria, housed in a beautiful historic adobe home; Luna Red (p. 164), with it's expansive yet intimate patio backed up the the San Luis Obispo Mission; and Novo Restaurant (p. 170) with it's award-winning late-night creekside dining. "We feel really blessed; I couldn't be more happy about living here and working on the Central Coast." Their success started from their very first venture in the early 80s: The Robin's Nest. From 1980–1984 The Robin's Nest stocked fresh produce from farmers' markets and served sandwiches, smoothies, and fresh juices. "Robin and I always had an affinity for health foods. We were vegan and vegetarian for some time before our son was born, and I had worked at a food co-op in the Bay Area. It was a nice, good fit for us to run the health food store in Cambria." They started hosting monthly dinners in the back room of the store, which inspired them to open Robin's Restaurant. "I want my guests to leave Robin's feeling that they have been well fed, both in body and spirit. Eating well is what we do. I love to be hospitable and I love to make people happy. When the restaurant is busy there is nothing quite like that energy," says Shanny. Robin's Restaurant is known for their creamy salmon bisque and for specializing in farm fresh, organic global fare. "We have something on the menu for everyone—from the vegetarian to the meat eater, small plates to large plates; we have it all!"

ROBIN'S RESTAURANT

WILLIAM OUDERKIRK

WHAT'S YOUR JOURNEY?

I knew since age 10 that I wanted to be a chef. I started my formal apprenticeship when I was 16. I'm originally from Canada, and moved to the United Kingdom at age 18 for culinary school and got an Advanced degree in Pastry. I worked at a high-end restaurant called Longueville Manor. We had 1 Michelin star, which put us in the Top 100 in the U.K., and we were rated in the Top 200 hotels in Europe. The property itself was 33 acres with 3 acres dedicated to the kitchen. We would plant the majority of what we used on the property itself. It was a very involved job, very fun! This is where I was really exposed to farm-to-table cooking. I then relocated to Connecticut to work with Master Chef Thomas Henkelmann for two years—he has 29 points on Zagat, which, there are only 11 restaurants in the United States with that rating. Then I went to Toronto to work at a place called Auberge de Pommier, which was my first Sous Chef position. We were rated #1 in the province for food, service, ambiance; we were in the Top 10 in the Canada and Top 50 in North America. After 3 years I decided that I wanted to travel, so I jumped on a Holland America Lines cruise ship and I went to over 50 countries in 18 months. It was a lot of traveling. One day you'd be in Tunisia, the next Malta, then Italy; all over the place! After 18 months I decided to move on—it was cold in Canada at the time so I picked California. Haha! I came to the Central Coast on vacation for 3 weeks and I really enjoyed it, so I decided to move here. I started out at Justin Winery for about a year in Paso Robles. Then I met Shanny (p. 178) in 2014 and Robin's Restaurant was a great fit for me, it was exactly what I wanted to do.

WOW! HOW DO YOU DESCRIBE THE FOOD AT ROBIN'S?

It's global cuisine. It's a very eclectic menu with something for everyone. It's great wholesome food with bold flavors and a rustic feel. It gives you that sense memory of home.

RUTIZ FAMILY FARMS

JERRY RUTIZ

HOW LONG HAVE YOU BEEN FARMING AND OPERATING THE FARM STAND?

The farm stand has been here for 11 years, and we've farmed on this property for 12 years. The previous 20 years, 1983–2003, I farmed on a different piece of property off of Huasna Road. During that time we didn't have retail sales, we just did 5–6 farmers' markets here in SLO County and 1 in Santa Monica. Since we moved onto this farm land, we only do 1 farmers' market per week year-round. We've been doing the Santa Monica farmers' market for 33 years now. We dropped all the other markets so that we could put all of our efforts into our local farm stand and weekly CSA box program. We know a good portion of our customers by their first name and we get to talk to them every week. We want the farm stand to feel like a community space; we host events and "u-pick" berry picking.

WHY DID YOU DECIDE TO KEEP THE SANTA MONICA FARMERS' MARKET?

Santa Monica is the largest in terms of sales; restaurants pre-order from us on a weekly basis and then they meet us at the market. On any given Wednesday, we have 25–35 different restaurant chefs that come to the market and buy from us. That's two thirds of our business—15 years ago this lucrative direct restaurant niche did not exist.

WHAT HAS BEEN A MONUMENTAL MOMENT IN YOUR FARMING CAREER?

A few years back we had a really hard frost here, and we lost everything for a couple of months. Several of the restaurants we sell to in Los Angeles did a fundraiser for us. They presented us with the check and I looked at the chefs and said, "Wow! This is amazing! We really appreciate this!" To which they replied, "Oh no, we really appreciate what *you* guys are doing as farmers."

SALLY LOO'S

JEN & BRANDON MANUELE

"I worked at a cafe in Santa Cruz and the owner taught me that a coffee shop is a 'Third Space'—you have your 'First Space,' which is your home, your 'Second Space,' which is your workplace, and your 'Third Space,' which is your safe space. It's important in a community to have those spaces—a community living room of sorts, where you feel at home. That is what we wanted when we opened our cafe," explains Jen Manuele. She and her husband Brandon lived in the quaint Railroad district neighborhood of SLO and had always wanted a place to eat brunch that had fresh organic eggs and really good food within walking distance. "We love organic food and working with farmers. It's always been in our heart and we wanted a place where we could do that." When the little cafe around the corner from their home went up for sale, they took the leap from being wedding photographers to make their dream a reality. Brandon shops at the markets every week and many farmers deliver straight to the cafe's back doorstep. "We are very blessed in SLO County—there is no excuse to not shop at farmers' markets. We love developing relationships with our farmers." What makes Sally Loo's so special is this personal connection to the local land, the tight-knit crew that works behind the counter, and the devotion that customers pour into this community-driven 'Third Space'—Sally's Loo's truly does feel like home!

SCOUT COFFEE CO.

SARA & JON PETERSON

"The catalyst for starting our own business was having our first daughter Lilly. I took 8 weeks off, then went back part-time, then full-time, then flex-time. It was really challenging because I had a really big job; I needed flexible hours and we needed more flexibility between the two of us. We both had high-level jobs at a small company (Verve Coffee Roasters in Santa Cruz) that was growing fast. Our original goal when we got married had always been to start our own business, and we decided to go all in with our savings. We thought—if we are going to do it, we have to do it now!" says Sara. She and her husband Jon own Scout Coffee Co. and their very own coffee roastery, HoneyCo Coffee Roasters.

"We are very motivated to *do*; we like to put things into action. Everyone has the same potential, it just depends on where you put your energy," explains Sara. "We have been working towards this goal for over a decade. Everybody thought we were crazy for starting a coffee shop—but this was our dream and we were determined," says Jon brightly.

This action-oriented power couple swiftly created a cult following for their liquid treats and baked goods. Everything is made from scratch, including their seasonal sodas (ginger lime, tangerine, strawberry and Meyer lemon), ever-changing milkshakes (olallieberry, honey lavender, strawberry buttermilk), and creamy almond milk (p. 20).

"Jon is very entrepreneurial and business-oriented, and I've always been very interested in food, hospitality, and creative outlets—we were able to to blend that all together to do something we truly love!"

SLO Creek Farms has been family-owned and -operated for over a decade. Blythe and Robyn Gable's 44-acre Certified Organic farm runs parallel to Highway 101, with SLO Creek running through the middle of their property. Their land includes a vegetable garden, community garden with 16 rentable plots, "u-pick" apple orchards, "u-pick" flower rows, and a pumpkin patch. Their apple orchard is one of the largest in the area with the majority of their apples being Braeburns. "Braeburns are great for eating, baking, saucing, and making cider," explains Robyn. Make sure to check out their incredible apple crisp recipe on page 108!

Every year the Gable family opens up their farm to host their annual harvest festival. Additionally, from September to December they participate in the Avila Apple Trail along with neighboring orchards, where folks are encouraged to explore the trail, pick fresh apples from fruiting trees, drink hard cider, and enjoy homemade apple pies. The Gable family is all about connecting and giving back to the community. Originally they started with a "u-pick", progressed to farmers' markets, hosted numerous classes on nutrition and grafting, partnered with Glean SLO (p. 192) and now they have connected with Cal Poly's Center for Sustainability. The Center for Sustainability helps to advance sustainability in the College of Agriculture, Food and Environmental Sciences (CAFES) through fundraising, outreach, and support for teaching and research. "We love the community. We embrace it. We are so thankful to be a part of it. We want everyone to be involved. We love what we do and we love having people come out to our farm!"

SLO CREEK FARMS
GABLE FAMILY

SLO GROWN PRODUCE & LONE OAK OLIVE OIL

PHILIP & NANCY LANGSTON

"I grew up in the Bay Area: Santa Clara, home of the semiconductor. My dad was an aerospace engineer; I've gone against family tradition!" laughs Philip Langston in his signature wide-brimmed hat, grinning from ear-to-ear. "I was a Crop Science Major at Cal Poly but I concentrated on greenhouse classes because I knew I wanted to go into controlled environment agriculture (CEA). I wanted to work for NASA and grow plants in space! My original senior project pitch was 'Seed Germination in Simulated Weightlessness', but it was rejected."

WHAT ATTRACTED YOU TO GREENHOUSE PRODUCTION AND GROWING HYDROPONICALLY?

With greenhouse production, you need to utilize as much of the volume of the greenhouse as you can, because your square footage is so expensive. My production is limited because I only have a half acre compared to everyone else's acreage. Scaling vertically allows me to increase production. Our hydroponic system works well for "two-dimensional plants," which refers to non-vining plants, like basil, that don't grow very tall. We sow the seeds in net pots, then drop it into the nutrient solution. There is no soil in this hydroponic system. The water gets filtered once and runs through the system over and over. It's a very efficient use of water and nutrients because instead of leaching into the ground or volatilizing into the air, it stays within the root zone.

WHAT DO YOU DO FOR PESTS?

Our pest control is all biologically based—we use insects to control other insects. We use ladybugs to control aphids on our basil and tiny parasitic wasps to control the whiteflies on our tomatoes.

TELL ME ABOUT YOUR AWARD-WINNING LONE OAK OLIVE OIL!

This recognition validates the balance in our flavor profile: a fruity nose and taste, slightly grassy on the palate and a mild pepper at the finish.

THE SPOON TRADE

JACOB TOWN "I lived in every town from Santa Maria to San Luis. My mom would always cook me artichokes; we used to eat them together by peeling them off and dipping them in mayo and butter while watcing movies—that was my introduction to cooking. I met both Brooke and Patrick at the Cracked Crab in 1999. I went to culinary school in San Francisco, did my externship at La Toque out in Napa, and ran that kitchen as the Sous Chef for 2 years. I worked at Gary Danko for 2 years—an amazing culinary breeding ground; then I went to Spruce—a Michelin star restaurant that serves locally sourced, farm-to-table fine dining. I was promoted to Sous Chef, ran their externship program, cheese program, did all the sauce making, and worked a station every single night. Next, I was the Executive Sous Chef at RN74 and became the Executive Chef at Piccino."

BROOKE TOWN "I went to The San Francisco Art Institute and I got a painting degree. While in Napa, I was a server at Rutherford Grill. When we moved back to San Francisco I became the Manager at NOPA and Nopalito. They both have quintessential farm-to-table models. They have the greatest relationships with their farmers and source from over 50 farms in the Bay Area. We always wanted to own our restaurant—it's been a 5 year goal for about 15 years, haha! We re-connected with Patrick, who was also living in the City at the time and working in the restaurant industry. We needed a trio to make a strong team—Jacob is the chef, my strengths lie in hospitality—Patrick was that third missing part."

PATRICK BERGSEID "I was the Manager at Pacific Catch for years, which started as 3 restaurants and then expanded to 6 by the time I left. It was awesome to work with a company that had strong values, and it wasn't always about the bottom line; it was really about living up to their values while still maintaining integrity during their growth. When I started brainstorming with Jacob and Brooke about The Spoon Trade, we wanted to create a casual yet refined neighborhood restaurant that you'd go get a burger and tall can or a nice bottle of wine with 3–4 courses. Those are the places I'm the most comfortable in—places where the food, wine, beer, and cocktails have integrity in them; places where you can tell the owners and workers there are having fun, too."

WHY THE NAME "SPOON TRADE"? "The spoon is the chef's paintbrush—most chefs have one in their pocket! Jake's been collecting or handing them out to his peers to instill a sense of pride in one's tools. It's about spooning food and trading stories; when you share food you usually pass around dishes and spoon a helping onto your plate. At the table you trade stories and share with your community; it's about bringing people together!" says Brooke.

Kelli "Sweet Pea" Castle is the young baking beaut behind Sweet Pea Bakery. Born and raised in Arroyo Grande, Kelli found her way back home to Arroyo Grande. after graduating from Sonoma State with a degree in Business Administration. Throughout her childhood and college years she spent hours recipe testing, refining her culinary skills, and developing her own unique twists on classic baked goods. One day the thought dawned on her, "...maybe I could make a business out of this." So, this passionate hobbyist-turned-entrepreneur decided to give it a go on her own. She started work-trading for and renting commercial kitchen space from Jeremy Davenport of Éclair Bakery (p. 156) so she could sell her baked goods at Rutiz Family Farms' farm stand (p. 180) on Fridays and sling her pastries to the masses at the local farmers' markets on Wednesdays and Saturdays. She quickly built up a cult following of Arroyo Grande villagers and tourists alike, and thus decided to start scouting the perfect location for her brick-and-mortar bakery. In the fall of 2013, Chef Brian Collins of Ember (p. 157) called Kelli to tell her about the vacant space next door to his soon-to-be-opened restaurant. With the help of family and friends she took the plunge in opening up Sweet Pea Bakery. Her cute bakery always has antique vessels and vases filled with fresh cut flowers. The walls are adorned with shabby-chic chalkboards with calligraphic quotes like "If you are afraid of butter, use cream!" and "Sometimes a cookie changes everything." She displays her treats in big apothecary-like glass jars, filled with the best kind of sweet, sugary medicine. "I got inspired to bake because I have a ginormous sweet tooth," she giggles. She is always experimenting and adding new flavor profiles to her large repertoire: strawberry Champagne tiramisu cakes, Crème de Menthe French-style *macarons*, apricot almond cranberry biscotti, fig and honeyed cream tarts, mixed berry pies, pumpkin scones with brown butter chai, *pain au chocolat*, pear gruyère croissants, chockablock cookies, Earl Grey madeleines, chocolate zucchini muffins—the list goes on and on!

TALLEY FARMS

ANDREA CHAVEZ

"My passion is to get people to eat more produce. I'm always interested in sharing good recipes of local, seasonal produce," says Andrea Chavez, Manager of the Fresh Harvest CSA program at Talley Farms. "Community Supported Agriculture is a way to actively support a local farm and the idea of eating seasonally. The original box—which is the best value—features 9–12 different items: 2–3 dinner vegetables, 2–3 kinds of fruit, and several salad items. We mix everything up each week." Talley Farms was founded by Oliver Talley in 1948, and is now owned and operated by second-, third-, and fourth-generation Talley family members. The Fresh Harvest program uses 40 acres of 1,400 total from Talley Farms. "The great thing about being part of the larger farm is that we can utilize all of the resources here: if we need more acreage, we can get it; if we need a bigger or smaller tractor, we can use it. The reason why our vegetables are so good, with such a long shelf life, is because everything is picked fresh and we are able to pre-cool the produce on-site." Andrea started the CSA program in the summer of 2012, which now has over 50 local pickup locations at schools, workplaces, and community centers. "Our boxes are so popular. We have over 4,300 subscribers, and we pack about 2,000–2,100 boxes per week. We can ship anywhere in California overnight." Great news for those who don't live nearby but still want the true taste of the Central Coast—it can now be delivered directly to your door! Fresh Harvest is extremely involved in the local community. "We supply produce to Arroyo Grande High School's P.E. classes. They are learning how to stay in shape, eat healthy, and cook seasonally. For homework each week they take a certain piece of produce home, learn how to cook it, write about it, and share their findings with the class. Every Friday Glean SLO (a program of the Food Bank Coalition of SLO) comes out to the farm, and they take our extra produce. It's a great partnership for us—they help harvest, prune, or take away extra produce and give it to those in need." To jump on the box bandwagon, visit *talleyfarmsfreshharvest.com*.

THOMAS HILL ORGANICS

CHRIS MANNING

WHAT'S YOUR BACKGROUND?
I'm from Montana. I grew up hunting, fishing, and both of my parents cooked at home. I had a feeling from a young age that I wanted to be a chef. After school I would make myself hash browns or eggs while watching Great Chefs of the West on PBS!

THE FOOD AT THO IS SO UNIQUE, HOW DO YOU DESCRIBE IT?
THO is California-French seasonal cuisine with a focus on fresh technique and sauces. I like to play around a lot with flavors and combos—I always cook with wine, so everything is really geared to be enjoyed with sparkling or still wine. I use a little extra acid, citrus, or vinegar for this reason, or really bright sauces. I'm classically French trained, but it's all about fresh, local, seasonal food with a global spin on it. I've been fortunate enough to travel a bit, so those places I visited have definitely influenced my cooking.

WHY IS SOURCING LOCAL AT FARMERS' MARKETS IMPORTANT?
Farm-to-table is important because it promotes local agriculture. It's really fun to go to the markets and really see where your food is coming from. It's awesome to see what has just been picked from the garden or ground. We love our farmers and are happy to support them!

Back in my college days, my gal pal Lauren and I used to ride our bikes downtown to the Thursday night farmers' market. Rain or shine, we'd always jerry-rig flats of strawberries from Y. Hayashi & Sons to the front basket of our rickety bicycles! *Interview with Alan Hayashi.*

CAN YOU TELL ME ABOUT YOUR FAMILY'S HISTORY?

My grandfather came over in the 20s from Japan. My father was born here in 1926. The "Y" in Y. Hayashi stands for Yeiju—that was my grandfather. "Y. Hayashi & Sons" refers to my grandfather and his sons (my father and my uncle). We are the Sons' sons and we've been on the ranch since we were kids. Three of us boys work on the ranch and two are well-respected surgeons. We all live in the area and are the third-generation here on the Central Coast. The farm was first started by my Dad, and to this day my Mom and Dad are still partners on the farm. I do a lot of the office admin work and man the fields, my brother runs the harvesting and planting, and my other brother handles the equipment. I've been in farming since I got back from college about 35 years ago. To this day, our area is the largest producer of bok choy and Napa cabbage in the nation. We used to be one of the biggest growers and shippers in the country through the Pismo Oceano Vegetable Exchange (POVE), but we have now scaled back in our production.

WHOA! WHAT CROPS DO YOU GROW NOW?

Throughout the year we grow broccoli, cauliflower, lettuce, leaf lettuces, Napa cabbage, bok choy, celery, bell peppers, squash, tomatoes, cucumbers, and of course, strawberries.

HOW LONG HAVE YOU OPERATED THE FARM STAND?

The farm stand began in the early 60s. At our roadside stand we sell a lot of our own produce, but we also source a lot fruits and veggies from the Central Valley, too.

880

THE FUTURE OF FOOD: FARMBOT & OPENFARM

My younger brother Rory Aronson is one of the most unique, intelligent human beings I've ever met—those that know him personally know this to be true. Growing up alongside him, I always knew he was destined to become a forward-thinking, entrepreneurial game-changer. A natural problem-solver, Rory was born with engineering in his blood—a chip off the old block (our dad is a mechanical engineer by trade)! He has maintained a curious mind that asks big questions and dares to answer them. He is now spearheading the innovation of hardware and software that will change the future of food!

WHAT IS FARMBOT AND OPENFARM?

FarmBot is an open-source automated precision-farming machine designed for small-scale, at-home DIY food production. It works very similarly to a 3D printer in that it moves in the XYZ space, but instead of printing plastic, it plants seeds, waters, and uses sensors to learn about the plants, the soil, and the environment. The owner of a FarmBot uses a web application to control and configure their device to grow exactly what they want and how they want it to be grown. If the owner of the FarmBot doesn't know how to grow food, that's okay—we are developing a database that describes how to grow different plants, with different practices, in different conditions. That database is called OpenFarm, which is also an open-source project built by a community of people all around the world. What we are hoping to do with FarmBot and OpenFarm is empower people to grow their own food in ways that they have never been able to do before, notably with precision, with agency, and at home with a small amount of time committed to the endeavor.

WHAT INSPIRED YOU TO START ALL OF THIS?

The FarmBot project and OpenFarm exist because of my frustration with trying to grow my own food. Home gardening takes a lot of time, expertise, and knowledge that I didn't really have available to me. So I decided to ask the question (and answer it): If food production were to be reimagined today—with today's technologies, consumer expectations, and abilities—what would it look like? The answer is open-source. The answer is community-driven. The answer is to give power back to the people. That's what we are trying to do with FarmBot and OpenFarm.

FOR THOSE WHO ARE UNFAMILIAR, CAN YOU EXPLAIN A BIT FURTHER WHAT "OPEN-SOURCE" MEANS?

Open-source is a lot of different things, but at it's core it's about sharing. It's about creating something and sharing that creation with others so that they can improve upon it, modify it, and then share it again in order to further humanity—rather than further one's individual personal gain.

WHERE DO YOU HOPE TO SEE FARMBOT IN THE FUTURE?

For FarmBot, I hope to see it become a global community of individuals and businesses, producing products, services, data, and everything else required that supports people in growing their own food. The FarmBot project is not just about building a consumer product, it's about rallying people behind the idea of at-home food production.

WHAT ARE YOUR HOPES FOR OPENFARM?

My hope for OpenFarm is that it becomes a self-sustaining community of software developers, designers, and content creators who are sharing how to grow food, as well as a global community who are learning how to grow food. I hope it becomes the Wikipedia for farming and gardening.

To learn more about FarmBot, humanity's open-source CNC farming machine, visit farmbot.io.
Want to learn to farm or garden with community created guides? Check out openfarm.cc.

RESOURCES

CENTRAL COAST GROWN

"Central Coast Grown creates strong connections among farmers, the public, and the land to nourish our community; supports local agriculture and makes local food products accessible for all."

centralcoastgrown.org

FARMSTEAD ED

"Our goal is to promote SLO County FARMsteading skills and practices via agricultural educational experiences, events, and gatherings at pop-up FARMsteading classrooms held at local farms, ranches and ag-related venues."

farmsteaded.com

EDIBLE SLO

"Edible San Luis Obispo celebrates the local, sustainable food sources of the San Luis Obispo area. Every season we serve up a combination of profiles, features, and recipes that illuminate the people who work so hard to bring this bounty to our tables. Intertwined throughout the magazine we include food as art through stunning photography and illustrations. Edible San Luis Obispo is a feast for the eyes, the intellect, and the palate."

edibleslo.com

GLEAN SLO

"GleanSLO is a program of the Food Bank Coalition of San Luis Obispo County that connects farmers and backyard growers with volunteers to harvest fruits and vegetables that would otherwise go to waste"

gleanslo.org

GROWING GROUNDS FARM

"Growing Grounds Farm of San Luis Obispo has offered compassionate and proactive treatment for adults suffering from mental illness. Using a combination of horticultural therapy and vocational training, the farm provides employment opportunities and a supportive environment for personal growth."

growinggroundsfarm.org

LOS OSOS VALLEY ORGANICS FARM'S CERTIFIED ORGANIC CSA

"Here at Los Osos Valley Organic Farm, we are passionately committed to bringing you the freshest, tastiest and best product we possibly can—and safeguarding Mother Earth while we do it. With a Certified Organic CSA, you not only get great food but you contribute directly to a healthy environment, too."

lovorganicfarm.com

RUTIZ FAMILY FARMS' FRIDAY HARVEST BOX

"An assortment of our most popular varieties are selected and boxed for you each Friday, available for pick-up only on Friday. No long term commitment, just order on a week-by-week basis using the order form in our weekly newsletter."

rutizfarms.com

SLO GROWN KIDS

"The mission of SLO Grown Kids is to improve the health and sustainability of the community through educational gardens, farm experiences, access to locally grown produce, and nutrition education integrated into core academic curricula."

slogrownkids.org

SLO PUBLIC MARKET AT BONETTI RANCH

"The Public Market's goal is to help cultivate the farm-to-table movement here in San Luis Obispo. Our plan is to attract local businesses to sell high-quality, local products delivered fresh daily. We aim to help connect city and farmers in a way that promotes social, economic, and cultural cohesion within our community."

slopublicmarket.com

SLO VEG'S FRUIT & VEGETABLE DELIVERY

"We are all about sustaining the local farmer and the local economy. Many of our farmers are pesticide-free and more are moving in that direction. The produce is less than 48 hours from being removed from the farmland."

sloveg.com

TALLEY FARMS' FRESH HARVEST PROGRAM

"Members may pick up their Fresh Harvest boxes at one of fifty different locations on the California Central Coast, or have a box delivered anywhere in California overnight directly to your home or business."

talleyfarmsfreshharvest.com

WINE CAMP

"Wine Camp is a communal food and wine experience on the Central Coast of California. Gather with us to discover local (Santa Barbara County to Monterey County) wines and provisions. Our wine and culinary adventures are authentic and simple, creative and intimate. Wine Camp celebrates the flavors of the season, the artisty behind winemaking, and the company we keep."

winecampcalifornia.com

FEATURED

ARTISAN
Paso Robles
artisanpasorobles.com

BAUTISTA FARMS
Arroyo Grande

BIG SKY CAFE
San Luis Obispo
bigskycafe.com

CAL POLY ORGANIC FARM
San Luis Obispo
aeps.calpoly.edu/cal_poly_organic_farm.html

DOMINGO FARMS
Arroyo Grande

ÉCLAIR BAKERY
Arroyo Grande
eclairbakery.com

EMBER RESTAURANT
Arroyo Grande
emberwoodfire.com

ESTHER'S GARDEN
Arroyo Grande

FOREMOST WINE CO.
San Luis Obispo
foremostslo.com

GOOD TIDES ORGANIC BISTRO
Los Osos
goodtides.com

JENSEN LORENZEN
San Luis Obispo
jensenlorenzen.com

JULIA'S JUICES
Grover Beach
juliasjuices.squarespace.com

LITTLE RED HEN BREAD
Arroyo Grande

LOS OSOS VALLEY ORGANICS FARM
Los Osos
lovorganicfarm.com

LUNA RED RESTAURANT • BAR
San Luis Obispo
lunaredslo.com

MAMA'S MEATBALL
San Luis Obispo
mamasmeatball.com

MAMA'S PRESERVES
Arroyo Grande
mamaspreserves.com

MEZE WINE BAR & BISTRO
San Luis Obispo
(now closed)

MT. OLIVE ORGANIC FARM
Paso Robles
mtoliveco.com

NEGRANTI CREAMERY
Paso Robles
negrantidairy.com

NOVO RESTAURANT & LOUNGE
San Luis Obispo
novorestaurant.com

OLD SLO BBQ
San Luis Obispo
oldsanluisbbq.com

PC CATTLE CO.
San Luis Obispo

PEPPER CREEK FAMILY FARMS
Arroyo Grande
www.facebook.com/PepperCreekFamilyFarms

RED BARN FARMS
Arroyo Grande

RINCONADA DAIRY
Santa Margarita
rinconadadairy.com

RIGHETTI RANCH
San Luis Obispo

ROBIN'S RESTAURANT
Cambria
robinsrestaurant.com

RUTIZ FAMILY FARMS
Arroyo Grande
rutizfarms.com

SALLY LOO'S
San Luis Obispo
sallyloo.blogspot.com

SCOUT COFFEE CO.
San Luis Obispo
scoutcoffeeco.com

SLO CREEK FARMS
San Luis Obispo
slocreekfarms.com

SLO FRESH CATCH
San Luis Obispo
(now closed)

SLO GROWN PRODUCE
Arroyo Grande
slogrownproduce.farm

THE SPOON TRADE
Grover Beach
thespoontrade.com

SWEET PEA BAKERY
Arroyo Grande
sweetpeabakeryag.com

TALLEY FARMS
Arroyo Grande
talleyfarms.com

THOMAS HILL ORGANICS
Paso Robles
thomashillorganics.com

Y. HAYASHI & SONS FARMS
Arroyo Grande
pove.net

INDEX

RECIPES BY TYPE

RECIPES BY SEASON

For more photos and products visit
slofarmersmarketcookbook.com